The Seventy Week Ministry of Jesus Christ:

Revelations from Restoring God's Sacred Calendar

by D. Michael Cotten

ISBN#: 978-0-9824802-7-4
©D. Michael Cotten
All Rights Reserved

Searchlight Press
Dallas, Texas
www.Searchlight-Press.com

The Seventy Week Ministry of Jesus Christ:

Revelations from Restoring God's Sacred Calendar

©D. Michael Cotten
All Rights Reserved

ISBN#: 978-0-9824802-7-4

No portion of this work may be copied in any manner whatsoever without written permission from the author, except in the case of brief quotations embodied in critical articles or reviews.

Contact Michael Cotten at:
DmichaelCotten@att.net

Searchlight Press
Who Are You Looking For?
5634 Ledgestone Drive
Dallas, Texas 75214-2026 USA
888-896-6081
www.Searchlight-Press.com

Manufactured in the United States of America

Dedication

I dedicate this book to my incredible family:

My brother, who started a second career dedicated to the Lord Jesus Christ, returned to college, and recently graduated from Perkins Seminary, Southern Methodist University;

My Father, who was an inventor, and who taught me not be afraid of starting something new;

My Aunt Frances, who wrote her last book at age 90;

My Grandfather, who was a missionary to the Spanish-speaking world, and started in Cuba.

D. Michael Cotten

The Seventy Week Ministry of Jesus Christ: Revelations from Restoring God's Sacred Calendar

Revelations from:
Daniel 9 – Seventy Sevens
Daniel 9 – Sixty-two Sevens
Jesus Christ – ministry 490 days
Three Passovers in John?
Birth Date of Jesus Christ
Birth Date of John the Baptist
Palm Sunday on the Sabbath
Last Supper is not Passover
Feast of Unleavened Bread
First Fruits offering
Jonah's Prophecy of three days & three nights
Resurrection on the Sabbath

And a daily look at the Ministry of Jesus Christ in the Harmony of the Gospels set with the Sacred Feast schedule, in the Sacred Calendar God devised.

The Seventy-Week Ministry, 5

New Revelations from
Rebuilding the Sacred Calendar

Part One: **Page 11**
Reconstructing GOD's Calendar reveals new truths in Daniel 9 Prophecies.

1. There is credible evidence the prophecies of the Bible have come to pass without fail.
2. There is credible biblical evidence the ministry of Jesus was not 3½ years.

Part Two: **Page 61**
The ministry of Jesus was seventy weeks in length, according to the prophecy in Daniel 9.

      Baptism
      Desert Experience
      Trip to Cana and Capernaum
      Trip to Jerusalem for The Feast of Passover, Unleavened Bread, and First Fruits.
      Map including first trip to Jerusalem for Feasts
      Early Judean ministry
      Trip to Sychar, to Cana to Nazareth and to Capernaum.
      Tour of Galilee
      Trip to Jerusalem for Feast of Shavuots (Pentecost)
      Map including second trip to Jerusalem for Pentecost
      Return Trip to Capernaum and Sea of Galilee
      Tour of Galilee and return to Capernaum for Feast

of Trumpets and Yom Kippur
Trip to Mount of transfiguration
Trip to Jerusalem for Feast of Tabernacles and sends out 70 disciples
Map including third trip to Jerusalem for Feast of Tabernacles
Teaching and healing in Judea and Perea
Trip to Jerusalem for the Feast of Dedication (Hanukkah)
Teaching and healing across the Jordan
Trip to Bethany to raise Lazarus from the dead
Passover is delayed one month because the barley is not ripe, so Jesus tours
Final trip to Jerusalem for Passover through Jericho and Bethany
The resurrection period and leading to ascension in forty days
Emanuel "GOD with us" sends the Holy Spirit to be "GOD in us"

Part Three: Page 151
Reconstructing GOD's Calendar reveals New Testament Truths

4. There is credible biblical evidence Jesus Christ followed GOD's Passion weeks schedule. **Page 154**
5. There is credible biblical evidence that the triumphal entry was not on Palm Sunday. **Page 166**
6. There is credible biblical evidence that the Last Supper was not the Passover Meal. **Page 182**

7. There is credible biblical evidence Jesus Christ was not crucified on Good Friday.
8 There is credible biblical evidence that Jesus was not resurrected on Easter Sunday.
9. There is biblical evidence that Jesus fulfilled the prophecy of Jonah of three days and three nights.
10. There is biblical evidence that Jesus offered the First Fruits offering as our High Priest.

Part Four: **Page 245**
11. There is biblical evidence that Jesus, The Messiah, was not born on Christmas.

Introduction
Part One:

The Lord Jesus Christ was a Jew and lived his life, without sin, subject to every law and commandment in the Torah. The "Matrix" of life and society in Israel revolved around: the agricultural harvests, GOD's Feasts, a burdensome Priesthood and Roman occupiers. The New Testament was translated into Greek by translators not familiar with the Feasts of GOD, not familiar with GOD's calendar, and not familiar with the Jewish society and the worship of one GOD.

The computer age has given Astronomy the knowledge to reconstruct "The Sacred Calendar," GOD's instructions for calculating weeks, months, years, seasons, and Feasts. This new knowledge has revealed new revelations in the Daniel 9 Prophecies about Jesus Christ Ministry and the world to come. The Lord's ministry is one of the layers within the Seventy sevens recorded in Daniel 9.

Part Two:
Detail of Jesus Daily movements: Using the harmony of the Gospels, set in the timing of The Sacred Calendar, this schedule tracks our Lord's daily movements from his Baptism to the giving of the Holy Spirit to the Disciples at Pentecost.

Part Three:
This reconstruction of "The Sacred Calendar" and the timing of GOD's Feasts allow us to understand the weeks surrounding The Lord's "Passion." This knowledge has added to our ability to measure, in precise time, the Daniel 9 Prophecies, and answer questions about the Lord's Ministry, down to the precise time he came onto the scene, died, was resurrected, and sat down at the right hand of the Father.

Part Four:
New dates of historical significance from reconstructing GOD's calendar discussed in this writing are:

    John the Baptist born on Passover

    Jesus Christ born on First day of the Feast of Tabernacles

    Jesus Christ circumcised on the Last Great Day ending Feast of Tabernacles

    Jesus Christ walks out of the wilderness experience on Aviv (Abib) 1, 27AD

    Daniel's Prophecy "Anointed One" coming 1st day of 1st month 483 years later

    Jesus Christ enters Jerusalem riding a colt on Nisan 10, 28AD

    Jesus Christ crucified on Passover Nisan 14, 28AD

    Daniel Prophecy Anointed One cut off in midst of 62 week Nisan 14, 28AD

    Jesus Christ in the Tomb Nisan 15, 28AD High Sabbath of Unleavened Bread

    Jesus Christ in the Tomb Nisan 16, 28AD

> Jesus Christ Raised at the end of Weekly Sabbath Nisan 17, 28AD
> Jesus Christ High Priest takes First Fruit offering to his Father Nisan 18, 28AD
> Jesus Christ's ministry of 490 days or Seventy sevens ends at the Feast of Pentecost.
> Israel becomes a Nation in one day on The High Sabbath of Pentecost.

The Old Roman Empire after AD 70 restricted and made illegal Jewish worship and Festivals to further complicate the importance of the Christian and Hebrew heritage.

Part One

Definitions and Terms

The most important part of the "Matrix" of time and life in the days of Jesus Christ were the Feasts of GOD (Yahweh) Five feasts having required attendance in Jerusalem for all men 13 and over and these feasts are to be celebrated forever. Exodus 12 and Leviticus 23.

Required Attendance in Jerusalem

1st Feast of the year: Passover celebrated on the 14th day of the month of Aviv (Nisan)

2nd Feast of the year: Unleavened Bread celebration starts on the 15th day of the Aviv (Nisan) Hebrew "Hag Hamatzah"

3rd Feast of the year: First Fruits celebrated on the first day of the week after the High Sabbath of Unleavened bread Hebrew name "Yom Bikkurim"

4th Feast of the year: Pentecost celebration starts on the 50th day after First Fruits Hebrew name "Shavuots"

Feasts Without Required Attendance in Jerusalem

5th Feast of the year: Trumpets (Yom Teruah) is celebrated at a time and day that no man knoweth. It happens at the sighting of the renewed moon starting the Sabbath month Tishri 1

6th Feast of the year: Yom Kippur celebrated on the 10th day of the Sabbath month of Tishri It is a day of Fasting and is the Day of Atonement when the sacrifice for the sins of the Nation of Israel is made.

Feasts With Required Attendance in Jerusalem
6th Feast of the year: Tabernacles (Sukkots) celebration starts on the 15th day of Tishri (Sabbath Month)

There are additional Feasts celebrated by the Jewish nation but these feasts are not ordered by GOD but instead these Feasts mark incredible moments in the history of the nation of Israel. The most famous of the Feasts is Hanukkah celebrated 75 days after Yom Kippur.

Months of the year
GOD did not name the months of the year except with the numbers 1 through 12 although the bible refers to the month of Abib (Aviv) the first month of the year. Aviv or Abib refers to the month starting with the sighting of the new moon when the barley crop will ripen. Sabbath Month is referred to the seventh month and includes the most Holy day, Yom Kippur (the day of Atonement), and the most Joyous of all the Feasts, Tabernacles (Sukkots). Because the Jews named the months, here is a listing of the Hebrew months:

1st month Nisan (Aviv or Abib)   7th month Tishri (Sabbath)

2nd month Iyyar   8th month Heshwan
3rd month Sivan   9th month Kislev
4th month Tammuz   10th month Teveth

5th month Av
6th month Elul

11th month Shevat
12th month Adar

Because the Sacred Calendar is based on lunar months 29.53 days per month every two or three years in the month of Adar when the barley is not ripe, a thirteenth month of Adar II will be added to await the (Aviv or Abib) barley crop and the next renewed moon.

Days of the Weeks

GOD did not name the days of the week except with numbers 1-7 but he called the Seventh day the Sabbath.

Parts of the days of the week: Israel followed the words of Genesis "And GOD saw that it was good. And there was evening and there was morning – the Third day." Therefore in the days of Jesus Christ, the day started at sundown when three stars could be sighted in the horizon.

Head of the Year

In Hebrew "Rosh Hashanah." Currently, the Jewish "Beginning of the year" is celebrated on the Day of Trumpets, but GOD told the Israelites to start the year at the sighting of the renewed moon in the month the barley was ripe. Exodus 12:1, 13:4

Some of the historical references to years are noted with a slash 3/2 because we are generally talking about years on the Julian Calendar that start at January 1 and The Sacred Calendar which starts around March /April, Therefore there is a difference in the starting of the year.

The Omer and the counting of the Omer

Leviticus 23:15-16, "And you shall count unto you from the morrow after the Sabbath from the day that ye brought the sheaf of the wave offering: seven Sabbaths shall be complete: Even unto the morrow after the seventh Sabbath shall ye number fifty days: and ye shall offer a new meat offering unto Yahweh" The Omer is used in counting the days and the Sabbaths between the First Fruits offering and the beginning of the Feast of Pentecost (fifty). This same counting is used to count between years of Jubilee.

Leaven

Leaven is used in bread used for peace offerings and not in the bread for burnt offerings. Leaven is used in Bread to make it rise. Leaven was used as a symbol for sin and therefore was purged from the home before Passover. Jesus said beware of the leaven in the Pharisees. Matthew 16:6-12 The Greek word for Leavened bread is "Artos" and that is the word used to describe the bread in the last Supper, the feeding of the 5,000 and the 4,000. The Greek word for Unleavened Bread is Azimos and is used when talking about the Feast of Passover and Unleavened Bread.

The Name Jesus Christ

Jesus Christ is translated from the Greek. "Jesus" is the name and the word for Christ is, "The Anointed."

The name Jesus Christ in Hebrew: *Yashua Hammessiach.*

Yashua is the name and *Hammaessiach* is "The Anointed".

There is evidence
That the Bible is the
Most exact foretelling of future
Events ever written.

The Bible is the only book that offers power and the "Words of life" by just reading and believing. The more of GOD's word you explore, the more amazed you will become at the incredible wisdom, choreography, and relevancy in every reading. The more you read and experience the more you realize The Bible has to be inspired by GOD in every detail. And he loved you enough to have it written, just for you.

Ecclesiastes 3:14-15. This is the gift of GOD vs.14 I know that everything GOD does will endure forever: nothing can be added to it and nothing taken from it. GOD does it so that men will revere him. Whatever is has already been, and what will be has been before, and GOD will call the past to account.

GOD's Word "was", and "is," and "will endure" forever. Studying GOD's Word will build our reverence for GOD and learning about the past will tell us about the future.

Example of GOD's incredible choreography.

Just imagine the likelihood that Chapter 117 of Psalms is the shortest chapter in the Bible, with two verses and that Chapter 119 of Psalms is the longest chapter with 176 verses. The middle of the bible is Chapter 118 of Psalms.

There are 594 chapters on each side of Chapter 118 and the 14th verse says, "The LORD *is* my strength and song, and is become my salvation."

If there had been just one more book added to the Bible or even one more chapter in the bible this choreography would not exist. My heart is warmed with love for a GOD that has given us incredible examples of watching out for his children. This choreography could only be an act of GOD.

Example of the relevancy of GOD's word.

After His resurrection, Jesus Christ, The Messiah, met the two Disciples on the road to Emmaus, They were dejected that Jesus had not been the one who was going to redeem Israel. Jesus said to them,

> "How foolish you are, and how slow of heart to believe all that the prophets have spoken! Did not the Christ have to suffer these things and then enter his glory?" And beginning with Moses and all the Prophets, he, Jesus, explained to them what was said in all the Scriptures concerning himself." (Luke 24:25)

GOD's word must be fulfilled or it isn't GOD's Word. Later that night (in the upper room) when all the disciples were together and the two disciples from Emmaus were telling of Jesus appearing, Jesus appeared in their midst and said,

> "Peace be with you" They were startled and

frightened thinking they had seen a ghost. Jesus said, "Why are you troubled and why do doubts rise in your minds? Look at my hands and my feet, it is I, myself, Touch me and see: a ghost does not have flesh and bones as you see I have." (Luke 24:37)

Jesus said to them,
> "This is what I told you while I was still with you: everything must be fulfilled that is written about me in the Law of Moses, the Prophets, and the Psalms." Then he opened their minds so they could understand the Scriptures. Jesus told them, "This is what is written: The Christ will suffer and rise again on the third day."

Then they remembered his words.

Jesus came to fulfill the Torah and the Prophets
Jesus said,
> "Do not think that I have come to abolish the Law (Torah) or the Prophets. I have not come to abolish them, but to fulfill them. I tell you the truth, until heaven and earth disappear, not the smallest letter, nor the least stroke of a pen will by any means disappear from the Law (Torah) until everything is accomplished." (Matthew 5:17-18)

What are some of the words of Torah and the Prophets that Jesus fulfilled?

Prophecies from the Old and New Testament.

There are over 300 messianic prophecies, more than 100 major Prophecies (See 17 below).

Shadow pictures of Jesus from the Tabernacles construction, materials, & furniture

Shadow pictures of Jesus from the Ark of the Covenant (Description below)

Shadow pictures of Jesus from the Priests garments

Shadow pictures of Jesus from the Feast of Passover, Unleavened Bread, & First Fruits

Shadow pictures of Jesus from the Feast of Pentecost

Shadow pictures of Jesus from the Feast of Trumpets, Atonement, & Tabernacles

Jesus Christ pictured in the Holy Furniture in the Temple

Jesus' life and words speak directly to the purpose of all the pieces of furniture in the Holy place, and Holy of Holies. There could have been chapters written on each of these relationships.

The Golden Candlestick or Menorah, used to illuminate the Holy Place, and Jesus Christ is the light of the world, John 1:5-10

The Table of Showbread and Jesus is the Bread of life, John 6:51

The Altar of Incense representing the prayers to GOD and Jesus Christ is sitting at the right hand of GOD our advocate with the Father and is well pleasing to GOD. Hebrews 4:14-16

The Laver of water used for water oblations and the Scripture says out of Jesus flow rivers of living water. John 7:37-39

The Ark of the Covenant is a wood box, indicating humanity, and covered in gold, indicating divinity, it is filled with the golden pot of manna, indicating the "Bread of Life," Aaron's rod that budded, indicating death, burial, and resurrection of our savior, and The Ten Commandments fulfilled in the life of Jesus Christ. The lid is gold with two Angels, one of on each end, of the "Mercy Seat," and the Shekinah Glory of GOD shone from between the angels. To fulfill one part of this "Shadow picture" when Mary enters the tomb of Jesus Christ, the Messiah, she is met with a living Angel on each side of the place where he laid, a perfect representation of the "Mercy seat." Could the negative image on the "Shroud of Turin" be caused from the glory of GOD present in the tomb at the resurrection moment?

Fulfillment of the Shadow Pictures Underlying the Feasts of GOD

Since the giving of the Torah, GOD's Feasts foretold in type and shadows the major redemptive works of Jesus Christ.

The first four feasts foretell Jesus Christ's first coming.
1. The Lord becomes the "Passover lamb that takes away

the sin of the world" in the Crucifixion,

2. The Lord is our sanctification pictured in each part of the Feast of Unleavened Bread. He is the sinless bread of Life shown in the Unleavened Bread, he suffered the stripes and piercing we see in the bread, he endured the vinegar, humiliation, spitting, and death on the cross.

3. The Glorification of Jesus Christ is seen in the resurrection and is the fulfillment for the Feast of First Fruits, and

4. The Commencement of the Church and the giving of the Holy Spirit and Power is the fulfillment of the Feasts of Pentecost.

The Fall Feasts of GOD
foretell the future coming of the Lord

Listed below are seventeen of more than three hundred Prophecies fulfilled about the "first coming" of Jesus Christ, the Messiah. These scriptures are part of the most well-known prophecies about the life, death, and resurrection of our Savior. There are many more fulfilled prophecies that will increase your faith and draw you closer to the Lord and reward you for studying the Bible.

1. Messiah to be born in Bethlehem: Micah 5:2
    fulfilled   Matt. 2:1-6, Luke 2:1-20
2. Messiah was to be born of a virgin: Isaiah 7:14
    fulfilled   Matt 1:18-25, Luke 1:26-38
3. Messiah, prophet like unto Moses: Deut. 18:15 18:19
    fulfilled John 7:40

4. Messiah, enter Jerusalem in Triumph: Zech 9:9
   fulfilled Matt. 21:1-9, John 12:12-16
5. Messiah, rejected by his own people: Isaiah 53:1
   fulfilled Matt. 26:3-4, John 12:37-43
   Prophesied again in Psalm 118:22
   fulfilled Acts 4:1-12
6. Messiah betrayed by one follower: Psalm 41:9
   fulfilled Matt 26:14-16, 47-50, Luke 22:19-23
7. Messiah to be tried and condemned: Isaiah 53:8
   fulfilled Luke 23:1-25, Matt 27:1-2
8. Messiah, silent before his accusers: Isaiah 53:7
   fulfilled Matt 27:12-14, Mark 15:3-4, Luke 23:8-10
9. Messiah struck and spat on by enemies: Isaiah 50:6
   fulfilled Matt 26:67, 27:30, Mark 14:65
10. Messiah mocked and insulted: Psalm 22:7-8
    fulfilled Matt 27:39-44, Luke 23:11,35
11. Messiah to die by crucifixion: Psalm 22:14,16
    fulfilled Matt 27:31, Mark 15:20,25
12. Messiah to suffer with criminals: Isaiah 53:12
    fulfilled Matt 27:38 Mark 15:27-28
13. Messiah's garments ownership: Psalm 22:18
    fulfilled Matthew 27:35
    chosen by casting lots: John 19:23-24
14. Messiah's bones not to be broken: Exodus 12:46
    fulfilled John 19:31-36
15. Messiah given vinegar for thirst: Psalm 69:21
    fulfilled Matt 27:34, John 19:28-30
16. Messiah to die as sacrifice for sin: Isaiah 53:5-6, 8, 10-12
    fulfilled John 1:29, 11:49-52: Acts 10:43, 13:38-39

17. Messiah to be raised from the dead: Psalm 16:10 fulfilled Acts 2:22-32, Matt 28:1-10

There are more than 300 prophecies about the Lord's first coming that could have been listed. One third of the entire Bible is prophecy. There are 900 prophecies about his next coming.

Open our eyes Lord we want to see Jesus
The entire Bible is rich with the wonders of GOD and the shadow pictures of The Messiah, Jesus Christ, who was and is, who came and will come again. When we see into the spiritual side of the world we can see GOD at work:
    Elijah raptured by the angels in chariots of fire in a whirlwind. 2 Kings 2
    The pillar of cloud by day and the pillar or fire by night Exodus 13:21
    Jacob's vision of the ladder going to Heaven with angels Genesis 28:10
    Nebuchadnezzar's vision of the Fourth man in the burning fiery furnace. Daniel 3:24-28
    Daniel's visited by Gabriel, the Angel who stands in the presence of Almighty GOD Daniel 9:20
    Moses seeing the hind parts of Almighty GOD Genesis 3 and signs in Genesis 4
    Zechariah's Angel visits, prophesies about his son, John the Baptist, & strikes him dumb. Luke 1
    Mary's visit from Gabriel to ask her about being the Mother of Jesus Christ. Luke 1
    Paul and John's revelation of Jesus Christ, Heaven,

and the future.

And many more

The most amazing of the fulfilled Prophecies (to the author) is Daniel 9. The very idea that the angel Gabriel tells Daniel the answer to his and the world's prayers is a series of events based on a series of numbers based on the perfect number 7. History helps us understand the first series is 483 years from the time of the decree for the rebuilding of Jerusalem until The Anointed One will begin his final stretch to fulfilling Prophecy of
    "putting an end to sin" and
    "bring in everlasting righteousness".

And when you read:
(1) Ezra 7:1: the timing is exact: "After these events, in the seventh year of the reign of Artaxerxes...Vs13 Now I decree that any of the Israelites in my kingdom, including priests and Levites, who wish to go to Jerusalem with you may go. Vs 9 He (Ezra) had begun his journey from Babylon on the first day of the first month. (The month of Aviv or Nisan) year 457 B.C. Do you think it is a coincidence that Artaxerses is the son of Esther, a Hebrew? The Hebrew language has no word for the word "coincidence".
(2) Matthew 3:13 John the Baptist telling Jesus, "I need to be baptized of you and do you come to me?" Jesus replied, " Let it be so now: it is proper for us to do this to fulfill all righteousness."

The First Layer of The Daniel 9 Prophecy
Daniel 9: Gabriel's words

"Seventy sevens (490) are decreed for your people and your holy city to:
> finish transgression,
> to put an end to sin,
> to atone for wickedness,
> to bring in everlasting righteousness,
> to seal up Vision and prophecy,
> to anoint the most holy.

"Know and understand this: From the issuing of the decree to restore and rebuild Jerusalem until the Anointed One, the ruler, comes there will be seven sevens and sixty two sevens.

"It will be rebuilt with streets and a trench but in times of trouble. After 62 weeks the Anointed one will be cut off and will have nothing."

The Fulfillment of
the First layer of Daniel 9 Prophecy
Daniel 9:24-26 The anointed one will come:
> 7 sevens and 62 sevens after the decree to rebuild Jerusalem goes forth.
> 49 years + 434 years = 483 years (Seven years left for the Tribulation)

Beginning point is Artaxerses decree to Ezra in Ezra 7:1

457/456 BC

The connection to our Lord:
> "483 years later Jesus Christ walks out of the Desert after 40 day fast and Satan's testing".
> Aviv (Nisan) 1, 27 A.D. 457/456 B.C.– 483 years + no year zero = 27 A.D.

Jesus walks out of the wilderness experience and John the Baptist remarks, to the Pharisees that came to question him, "Behold the Lamb of GOD that takes away the sin of the world"

Fulfillment of the
Second Layer of The Daniel Prophecy

There has to be a second layer to the Daniel Prophecy because of the announcement that the Anointed One will be cut off after 62 weeks and have nothing. Further investigation into the timing of the ministry of Jesus Christ reveals, "From the Baptism of Jesus Christ, by John the Baptist and the anointing by GOD, to the giving of the Holy Spirit at Pentecost is 490 days or 70 sevens."

And from the Baptism and Anointing, the beginning of Jesus Ministry to the Crucifixion is 62 weeks. Four days to the Crucifixion and three days to the Resurrection of Jesus Christ, and 7 sevens later Jesus Christ baptizes the Disciples and others with the Holy Spirit and Fire at Pentecost and the Church age begins.

This chronology fits with GOD's calendar and with the following:
> The Baptism and Anointing of Jesus as the High Priest Luke 3:22-23
> The Feasts schedule, and
> with Luke 3 (Jesus is 30 years of age) and John 2:20 (year 27/28)and

And is the Fulfillment of Daniel 9:
> Christ is cut off in the midst of the 62nd week and has nothing.
> From the Baptism of Jesus Christ, The Messiah, it is 490 days or 70 sevens later,

Jesus Christ baptizes the Apostles with the Holy Spirit and fire on Pentecost

Jesus did not need to be Baptized, but the New High Priest must be washed or immersed (Mikvah) in water and anointed to begin service in the new Priesthood after the order of Melchesidek. After the cleansing ritual and the anointing of GOD with the Spirit, Jesus Christ as "The High Priest" is ready for service in the Temple. This cleansing ceremony must be administered by a priest, and John the Baptist was a priest out of the line of Aaron who had been set apart by GOD for this work. John 1:32 and Exodus 29:4-9

There has to be a third layer and fourth layer to the Daniel Prophecy because there are seven years left to be completed and the Temple must be rebuilt so that the abominations of desolation can be offered by the anti-christ.

Possible, plausible, and startling revelation for the third layer of Daniel 9
The Setting

May 14, 1948: On Saturday, The Sabbath, invitations went out for the Ceremony to Proclaim Independence of Israel at the Tel Aviv Museum. The invitations went out at 10:00 in the morning for late in the afternoon so as to not conflict with the Sabbath (Saturday May 14,1948)

Converting the 1947/1948 Gregorian calendar to the Sacred Calendar

According to GOD's Sacred Calendar, sundown May 14, 1948 begins the next day, the 6th day of Sivan (Hebrew 3rd month) which is the 50th day of counting of the omer, the High Sabbath of Pentecost (Shavuots).

Note: the Rabbinic calendar in use in Israel in 1948 recorded an extra month of Adar in 1947. The calculations for this decision are not based on barley crop grown in the Jerusalem area but instead on an arithmetic calculation of the extra month (7 times in 19 years) by the Rabbi's.

Using GOD's sacred calendar, without the Rabbi's arbitrary calculation, Israel became a nation on the High Sabbath of Pentecost, in one day.

Rebirth of Israel in one day

Isaiah 66:8 Who has ever heard of such a thing? Who has ever seen such things? Can a country be born in a day? Or a nation be brought forth in a moment? Yet no sooner is Zion in labor than she gives birth to her children....

Vs. 10 Rejoice with Jerusalem and be glad for her, all of you who love her: Rejoice greatly with her.

Note: the Seventy sevens, 490 day ministry of Jesus Christ, The Messiah, ended on the Sabbath before the High Sabbath of Pentecost. The Nation of Israel was birthed on the High Sabbath of Pentecost, the day after the Lord baptized the disciples and converts with the Holy Spirit and fire 1920 years before.

Does it seem more important to understand GOD's calendar?

I cannot say that the Lord has spoken to me and informed me of a specific order of his next coming, but he has told me to pay attention to the signs of the times and to be ready! Also, the patterns are here for the "last seven years" in the Daniel prophecy to begin.

To date, the fulfilled prophecies of Daniel 9 and Isaiah 66:8 are:
>The decree to rebuild Jerusalem went forth on the first day of the first month in 457 BC.
>The Anointed One came on the scene on the first

day of the first month 483 years later.

The Anointed One was cut off and had nothing in the midst of the 62nd week on Passover.

The Anointed One baptizes disciples with the Holy Spirit & Fire 490 days (70 sevens) after his baptism.

The Anointed One baptized the Disciples with the Holy Spirit on the Sabbath starting the Feast of Pentecost.

The Nation of Israel was reborn in one day in 1948 AD on the High Sabbath of the Feast of Pentecost one day later in the Feast schedule than the giving of the Holy Spirit in 28AD.

Yahweh has given us dates for all his Feasts, "but one", the Feast of Trumpets.

> The Feast of Passover is celebrated on 14th day the Month of Aviv (Abib)
>
> The Feast of Unleavened Bread is celebrated on 15th to the 21st day of Aviv
>
> The Offering of First Fruits is celebrated on First day of the week after Passover
>
> The Feast of Pentecost is celebrated 50 days after First Fruits offering.
>
> The Feast of Trumpets is celebrated on a day and hour no man knows
>
> The Feast of Yom Kippur is celebrated on the 10th day of Tishri
>
> The Feast of Tabernacles starts on the 15th day of Tishri

Jesus has fulfilled the Spring Feasts Of GOD (Passover, Unleavened Bread, First Fruits, & Pentecost)

The next Feast of GOD in Daniel 9 is the Feast of Trumpets, the Feast that is celebrated on a day and hour no man knoweth, because it is started with the sight of the renewed moon in the Sabbath month (Tishri) of the year. The Trumpets sound through out the Land and call everyone to a Sabbath Day, a day without work. Psalm 81 is called the Feast of Trumpets Psalm.

Do you think Jesus was speaking of returning on the Feast of trumpets in I Thessalonians 4:16?
> For the Lord, himself, will come down from heaven with a loud command, with the voice of an Archangel, and with the trumpet call of GOD and the dead in Christ will rise first. After that we who are alive and are left will be caught up together with them in the clouds to meet the Lord in the air. And so we will be with "The Lord" forever. (I Thessalonians 4:16)

Jesus also says in Matthew 24:36:
> But of that day and hour knoweth no *man*, no, not the angels of heaven, but my Father only.

Daniel's prophecy and the patterns from Daniel give us possibilities to consider and spark our anticipation. But I am not saying that the signs are telling us when Jesus is coming for his church.

Paul, the Apostle, tells the people in Thessalonika (I Thessalonians 1:10) in Philippi (Philippians 3:20), and in Corinth (II Corinthians 4:13-14) that there are no restrictions for Jesus to come for his Church from the time of Paul until today. We need to watch the sky for the coming of the Lord in the Heavens with the sound of the trump an event for which there has not been any conditions. There are conditions for the beginning of the Seven years of Tribulation.

The pattern of the Feasts of the Lord and the prophecy of Daniel would indicate the fulfillment of the prophecies could be close at hand for the last seven years of the Daniel prophecy.
> 63 years from the rebirth of Israel in 1948 + 63 years = 2011
> 70 years from the rebirth of Israel in 1948 + 70 years = 2018

The rebuilding of the third Temple in Jerusalem and the total demise of Damascus are two prophecies that happen before or during the last seven years of the Daniel 9 prophecy, but the timing of Jesus Christ coming for his church has no remaining requirements.

The Temple rebuilding groups have started:
> Training Priests in the elements of sacrificing,
> These Temple groups have rebuilt the sacred Temple furniture and altars,
> The nine red heifers are ready for the purification

of priests and the Temple.

Several architectural plans have been made and negotiations are ongoing to unify the Jewish sects into a cohesive group behind building the new Temple.

Dr. Asher Kaufman of the Hebrew University has established the positioning of the first and second Temples on the Temple Mount in relation to the Eastern Gate and can confirm from his own archeological excavations that the third Temple can be built and when completed be 80 feet from the Dome of the Rock Mosque.

Conclusion: Allow GOD's word to speak to you, marvel in the incredible perfection of its fulfillment, allow your relationship with GOD to fill you to overflowing, and give the love, GOD gave you, away to a lost and dying world.

What biblical evidence Supports, The Messiah, Jesus Christ having a Three and one half year Ministry

There is no credible evidence that Jesus Christ ministry was 3.5 years and there is convincing evidence that the ministry of Jesus Christ was 490 days or 70 sevens which agrees with the Daniel 9 prophecy of our Savior.

To Begin:
God Almighty has given us a calendar. Is it a wonder that we are trying to date events of GOD and failing with the Gregorian, Julian, Syrian, Rabbinic, Prophetic, and other calendars? GOD's reckoning of time is simple.

1. Rosh Hashanah (The Head of the Year) shall start with the new moon in the month that the Barley is (Aviv) ready to harvest. (Exodus 12:1)

2. If the barley is not ready to harvest (Aviv) then there shall be a thirteenth month added to await the next new moon and Aviv (Abib) Barley. (Exodus 23:14)

That is it, that is the system and it cannot fail.

This is the system in use in Jerusalem during the ministry of Jesus Christ and the Apostles. After 70 A.D. Rosh Hashanah was changed by the Pharisees after the sacking of the Temple to be the beginning of the Sabbath month because the Priesthood could no longer know when the barley was ripe in Israel and broadcast the information to the dispersed Nation of Israel.

The lunar cycle is 29.5306 day months, in the sacred calendar. The month can only be 29 or 30 days, not 28 or 31, because the .5306 part of each lunar cycle will always create a new day every other month. Therefore in a twelve-month year there are 6 months of 29 days and 6 months of 30-day months or a total of 354 days, leaving 11.25 days short of the Solar year of 365.25 days. Every two to three years there is a thirteenth month of Adar.

When Israel did not have the Temple, the leadership decided to have the thirteenth month happen in nineteen year cycles with the leap year being the third, sixth, eighth, eleventh, fourteenth, seventeenth, and nineteenth year. Now that Israel is a Nation in its homeland they are beginning to plant Barley to be able to use GOD's calendar.

The week is 7 days in every part of the world, every culture, every ethnicity, every religion. Except that GOD set it up that way for his Children, there is no good reason for the week to be 7 days in length. For other ethnicities and religions, why not ten days or five days, five divides into 30 and 365 making annual calculations easy.

However, the week is the centerpiece of GOD's Sabbath Cycle. Every multiple of 7 is used to bring us closer to

GOD and it seems GOD set it up for our best interests. Can you imagine living without weekends?

(Exodus 20:9) Six days shall thou labor and do all thy work: vs. 10 But the seventh day is the Sabbath of the Lord thy GOD: in it thou shall not do any work, you nor your son, your daughter, your manservant, your maidservant, nor your cattle or the stranger in your gates. Vs 11 For in six days the Lord made heaven and the earth, the sea and all that is in them and rested on the seventh day: wherefore the LORD blessed the Sabbath day and Hallowed it.

The 24 hour day was started at a time approximating sundown and the sighting of three stars. Israel counted the day parts in this fashion because after each act of creation the scriptures say, "And GOD saw that it was good. And there was evening and there was morning the third day. Genesis 1:13 Therefore in Israel in the time of our Lord the day started at the sighting of three stars approximately dusk or sundown.

Reasons The Sacred Calendar is important
The Bible uses the Sacred Calendar to make a record, time, and date important events and if we don't use GOD's Calendar, how can we expect to confirm dates from GOD's word:
> (Genesis 7:11) In the six hundredth year of Noah's life, in the second month, and on the seventeenth day of the month, that very day all the springs of

> the great deep burst through and the sluices of heaven opened, and a heavy rain fell on the earth for forty days.
> (Zechariah 7:7) On the twenty fourth day of the eleventh month of Shebat, in the second year of Darius, the word of the Lord came to the prophet Zechariah, son of Berekiah, the son of Iddo.
> (Exodus 12:40) The time the Israelites spent in Egypt was four hundred and thirty years. And on the very day the four hundred and thirty years ended all Yahweh's armies left Egypt.

These are three scriptures, among many, that underscore our need to know the Sacred Calendar. It is now possible to reconstruct more of the History of Jesus Christ because NASA and other Astronomy groups can give us the sighting of the renewed moon, in Jerusalem, back to the beginning of recorded time and beyond. The only variable is which year to add the addition of the thirteenth month to adjust the lunar and the solar year. Approximately once every three years.

The Prophets also give compelling reasons to know the Sacred Calendar in
> (Amos 3:7) Surely the Sovereign Lord does nothing without revealing his plan, to his servants the prophets. Since this revealing of GOD's plan is always in the future, it is very important to know the Sacred Calendar.

When Daniel was praying in the 68th year of the captivity: Jeremiah prophesied 70 years of captivity.
> (Daniel 9:1) In the first year of Darius, son of Xerxes, who was made ruler over the Babylonian kingdom. In the first year of his reign, I, Daniel understood from the Scriptures, according to the word of the Lord given to Jeremiah, the prophet, that the desolation of Jerusalem would last seventy years.

In John 16:12, Jesus says,
> I have much more to say unto you, more than you can bear, but when he The Spirit of Truth comes, he will lead you into all truth. He will not speak on his own, he will speak only what he hears and he will tell you what is YET TO COME.

Dating Jesus Christ's Ministry

Note: If Jesus had a three and one half year ministry, there would be 10 required trips to Jerusalem to meet with GOD at the appointed Feasts. Each of the disciples would also be required to go to Jerusalem to the Temple, so everyone would be seeing each other, (Including 3 of the four Gospel writers). The Gospels only report four trips to the Appointed Feast required by GOD during the ministry of Jesus Christ.

The date with the most credibility of all the dates available to date the Lords age and ministry is from John 2:20, about two months after his Baptism and Anointing. Jesus attended the Passover Feast. He discovered merchants selling in the Temple, and he made a whip of cords and cleansed the Temple of merchants and their merchandise and was then confronted by the Priests. The Priests and Pharisees said, "What miraculous sign can you show us to prove your authority to do all this"? Jesus answered them, "Destroy this Temple and I will raise it again in three days" The Jews replied, "you are going to rebuild the Temple in Three days and it has taken 46 years to build this Temple." But the Temple he had spoken of was his body. The Temple was started in 19/20 B.C. Therefore this Passover Feast was in the year 27 A.D. Therefore this date "27AD" is a marker for all timing sequences of the historicity of Jesus Christ.

The most important connective date to establish The Messiah, Jesus Christ age and ministry start is from Luke's Gospel. Luke 3:23 when all the people were being baptized. Jesus was baptized too....vs.23 Now Jesus himself was about thirty years old when he began his ministry."

The Greek word "about" here is "hosei", meaning near but not yet attained. Not "peri", the Greek word for about, vicinity, a much broader term.

What a difference a year makes!

The year of the crucifixion and resurrection must be and is 28 AD. To fulfill all the prophecies and fit inside the timing markers listed in Luke, the sighting of the renewed moon must be on the fourth day of the week, so that Passover is on the fourth day of the week, three days and nights before the end of the weekly Sabbath.

Dating must also line up with Requirements of the Torah and the Prophets:

(1) The Messiah, Jesus Christ, has to fulfill all the prophecies, requirements of the Torah, and the shadow pictures of the Feasts.

(2a) The priest is available for service when he reaches thirtieth year. To fulfill the shadow pictures of the Old Testament (Numbers 4:47), Jesus started his Ministry about age thirty (Luke 3:23).

(2b) The High Priest must be baptized (Mikvah) and anointed to begin his ministry. Exodus 29:4-9 Matthew 3:13-15 "Let it be so now for it is proper for us in this way to fulfill all righteousness". John describes the anointing in John 1:32.

(3) The Passover Lamb must be a male lamb of the first year without spot or wrinkle. To fulfill the Passover Feast and the First Fruits offering. Jesus must be crucified before the end of his 31st year.

(4) Exodus 23:14 Three times a year you will hold a feast in my Honor.....Vs.17 Three times a year your men folk will appear before Lord ......Vs.18 You will bring the best of the first fruits of your soil to the House of Yahweh your GOD. To fulfill GOD's requirement of meeting with him 3 times a year in Jerusalem.

If you hold with the 3 plus year ministry of Jesus Christ, the synoptic Gospels must reconcile ten trips to Jerusalem, or we must assume the Gospel writers lost Jesus for two years or we must reduce the number of Feasts of the Lord during the ministry of Jesus. The Messiah was in Jerusalem every time his Father required attendance to the Feasts as recorded in the Torah or he can't be our Savior.

(5) Messiah must be born in Bethlehem where all the Passover lambs are raised. And prophecy dictates. (Micah 5:2)

(6) The Messiah, the Anointed one, (Daniel 9) must enter the scene on the first day of the first month in 27 AD exactly 483 years after the decree for Ezra to leave Babylon to rebuild Jerusalem on the first day of the first month of 457 BC. (Ezra 7:9) It must be this year to line up with Jesus being 30 years of age and be in the right relationship to the age of the Temple from John 2:20

(7) Hebrews 6:19-20 We have this hope as an anchor for the soul, firm and secure. It enters the inner Sanctuary (Holy of Holies) behind the curtain, where Jesus, who went before us has entered on our behalf. He has become a High Priest forever in the order of Melchisedek.. Therefore Jesus must live up to the demands GOD put on the priesthood.

The most confusing Scriptures to the timing of the Ministry of Jesus Christ, The Messiah.

The New Testament scriptures that allows there to be any assumption that Jesus had a three-year ministry are the three references to a Passover in the Gospel of John. When the original texts are studied, not all of the very oldest manuscripts have these eight words, "and the Feast of Passover was drawing nigh".

How can we reconcile, using biblical evidence, the four Gospels and their timing of the Feasts of Yahweh and the timing of events in the harmony of the Gospels? John is the only Gospel with the first Passover. None of the other Gospels have a Passover until the Passover, when our Lord was crucified. What logical timing of events in Matthew, Mark, and Luke would indicate a Fatal error in John 5:1 and 6:4.

>John 2:13 starts the first Passover of the Gospels
>John 5:1 characterizes Jesus going to Jerusalem for a Feast of the Jews, but these are the "Feasts of GOD" The timing would work as it does in the other Gospels to be the Feast of Pentecost (Shavuots). In the Greek, there are references to "THE" Sabbath and "A" Sabbath. This lineup of days happens every Pentecost where a high Sabbath follows the 49-day of counting the Omer or the day after the seventh Sabbath and the next day is the High Sabbath of Pentecost. 5:9, 5:10, & 5:16 The words in Greek are different referring to a High Sabbath and weekly Sabbath.

All four Gospels have the feeding of the five thousand and

then three of the Gospels head to Jerusalem for the Feast of Tabernacles but John 6:4 has Jesus going to the Feast Of Passover, but the eight words "and Passover the feast of the Jews was near" is not in all the oldest Greek transcripts and is a bad translation because Passover has never been a Feast of the Jews it is a Feast of Yahweh. The Feast of Trumpets and Yom Kippur are feasts that don't require a trip to Jerusalem and they both happen within two weeks of the Feast of Tabernacles and would fit with the feeding of the 4,000 and 5,000 with leavened bread.

John 7: Jesus is going to the Feast of Tabernacles. If John were correct in vs.6:4, then Jesus did nothing worth recording for nearly an entire year. But if like the other Gospels John 6 is the Feast of Trumpets or Yom Kippur, then all the Feast are in order and Jesus went to all the Feast as required by GOD.

John 9: Has Jesus going to, the Next Feast, Hanukkah, Feast of Lights (not a mandatory attendance in Jerusalem). Jesus, The Messiah is there to fulfill the shadow picture of the Feasts of Lights. The "Light of the World", is at the Feast of Lights.

The Triumphal Entry of Passover week begins in John 12:12 .
The harmony in all the Gospels can help us to determine when something is out of order. The translators for the New Testament were fluent in Greek but not necessarily knowledgeable in The Feasts of Yahweh, or the translators

would not have called them the Feasts of the Jews, and would not be so disrespectful as to not capitalize Passover. Therefore when you eliminate the fatal errors from the phraseology in John it is easy to see that Jesus Christ, The Messiah, was in Jerusalem every time his Father required men over thirteen to be there.

Teachings of Jesus Christ, The Messiah, that indicate the timing of John 6:4 is The Feast of Trumpets followed by Tabernacles not Passover.

The bread of Life discourse in John 6 is topical of the Fall Feast of the Lord because three times the Lord mentions "and I will raise him up in the last day" (verses John 6:39, 40, & 54 which is a theme of the prophecies associated with the Fall Feasts of the Lord). This fact further shows the likelihood that John 6:4 is translated incorrectly and this passage refers to The Feasts of Trumpets, Yom Kippur, Tabernacles and not Passover.

What do we know about the Feasts of GOD in John 6:4 that would be a fatal error to this Feast being Passover?
1. Attendance is required in Jerusalem at Passover by GOD and Jesus is not going to Jerusalem as written in Exodus 12:2. Jesus would not be keeping 5,000 men from traveling to Jerusalem if Passover is near as mentioned in John 6:4 The Feast of Trumpets and Yom Kippur do not require attendance in Jerusalem.

2. Bread made with Leaven must be burned before the

Passover Meal and the Feast of Unleavened Bread

Leviticus 23:4 These are the Lord's appointed feasts, the sacred assemblies you are to proclaim at their appointed times. The Lord's Passover preparation starts on the tenth day of the month and Passover meal begins at twilight on the fourteenth day of the first month. On the fifteenth day of that month the Lord's Feast of Unleavened Bread begins for seven days, you must eat bread made without yeast, On the first day hold a Sacred assembly (High Sabbath) and do no regular work. ….And on the seventh day hold another Sacred assembly (High Sabbath)

If John's Gospel is correct and the other Gospels wrong, Jesus would be feeding the 5,000 and later 4,000 with leavened barley loaves during the feast of Passover and Unleavened Bread (azimos), because the word used in the feeding of the 4,000 and the 5,000 is the word for leavened bread (artos).

Therefore John 6:4 cannot be Passover, not even a year later, because a year later he will still be required to be in Jerusalem and he will not be eating leavened bread at the Feast of Unleavened Bread. The translators have been exposed for not being familiar with the Feasts of GOD their schedule and their requirements.

**Hebrew Dates in the Sacred calendar for
The Ministry of Jesus Christ, the Messiah, and
Required trips to Jerusalem for the Feasts of GOD.**

(1) Starts with his Baptism and Anointing
This date was arrived at by calculating the distances traveled, 40 day wilderness experience, and Sabbaths in reverse order from Rosh Hashanah.
Baptism and Anointing of Jesus on the 19 day of Shevat 26AD
Baptism of Jesus Christ by John the Baptist and Anointing by GOD with the announcement this was his "Beloved Son."

(2) Fulfills prophecy of Daniel 9 concerning the Anointed one entering the scene 483 years on the exact day, month, and year prophesied.
Aviv 1, 27 A.D. End of the 40 day wilderness experience and fast and then the testing.
Rosh Hashanah, the Head of the year, The first day of the first month of the year 27AD.
John 1:29 Jesus walks out of the wilderness and John the Baptist remarks to Pharisees from Jerusalem "Behold, the Lamb of GOD that takes away the sin of the world."
(Note: these words were not spoken at the baptism, but when John the Baptist was describing Jesus to bystanders.)

(3) Aviv 10, 27 AD Jesus Christ first trip to Passover after age 30. Map #1
John 2:20 The Jews replied, It has taken 46 years to build this temple and you are going to raise it in three days.(AD 27)

(4) Sivan 8, 27AD   Trip to Jerusalem for GOD's Feast of

Pentecost (Shavuots) Map #2
(5) Tishri 15, 27AD Trip to Jerusalem for GOD's Feast of Tabernacles (Sukkots) Map #3
(6) Kislev 25, 27AD Trip to Jerusalem for Feast of Chanukah (Lights) Map #4
(7) Nisan 10, 28AD Trip to Jerusalem for GOD's Feast of Passover, Unleavened Bread and First Fruits. Map #4

The importance of the Crucifixion on the fourth day of the week is another fulfillment of GOD's Shadow pictures. The Jewish wedding last for a week and virgins are married on the fourth day of the week and widows on the fifth day of the week.

(8) The Year 28AD or 4030 is important because "The head of the year" is the fourth day of the week and therefore:

> The Triumphal entry is on the tenth day of the month and is the Sabbath
>
> The Passover is the fourteenth day of the month and fourth day of the week
>
> The High Sabbath of Unleavened Bread is on the fifteenth day of the month and the fifth day of the week.
>
> The weekly Sabbath is on the seventeenth day of the month
>
> The First Fruits offering on the first day of the week and the eighteenth day of the month.
>
> Each and every date and required action happens as GOD appointed.

(9) Sivan 8, 28AD Resurrection period Trip to Jerusalem for GOD's Feast of Pentecost

When the Calendar of Feasts happens in harmony with all the Gospels then the Daniel 9 Prophecies offer a new look at the timing of the ministry of Jesus, The Messiah.

The new layer in the Daniel 9, Seventy week prophecy, answers the age-old problem for Theologians of what to do with The Anointed One being cut off in the midst of the 62nd week and have nothing. Also answers the question why did GOD need to be baptized? He did not need to be baptized unto repentance, but he needed to be washed (Mikvah) and anointed to enter the new priesthood and start the count for the sixty two sevens. Exodus 29:4-9 John 1:32

Daniel 9:24-26
"Seventy sevens (490) are decreed for your people and your holy city to
> finish transgression,
> to put an end to sin,
> to atone for wickedness,
> to bring in everlasting righteousness,
> to seal up Vision and prophecy and (not fulfilled yet and described in Daniel 12)
> to anoint the most holy.

"Know and understand this: From the issuing of the decree to restore and rebuild Jerusalem until the Anointed One, the ruler, comes there will be seven sevens and sixty two sevens. It will be rebuilt with streets and a trench but in times of trouble. After 62 weeks the Anointed one will be cut off and will have nothing.

Fulfillment of the First Layer of Daniel

The Pharisees and teachers of the law were questioning John the Baptist when the Messiah, Jesus Christ walked out of the Desert experience after 40 day fast. The Jews were in the desert for 40 years before entering the Promised Land.

John 1:29 The next day John saw Jesus coming toward him and said, "Look the Lamb of GOD, who takes away the sin of the world". This is the one I meant when I said, "A man who comes after me has surpassed me because he was before me". This event happened on Rosh Hashanah two weeks before Passover, Unleavened Bread, and First Fruits.

Aviv 1, 27 A.D. 457 /456 B.C. – 483 years + the year zero = 27 A.D.

The Second Layer of The Daniel Prophecy must deal with the 62 sevens after the appearance of the Anointed One. The evidence shows that the prophecy of the Anointed One being cut off and having nothing after 62 sevens must fit within the ministry of Jesus Christ. The Total ministry of Jesus Christ from the Baptism by John to the giving of the Holy Spirit at Pentecost is 490 days or Seventy Sevens.

A. 62.5 weeks from the Baptism of Jesus Christ, The Messiah, to the Crucifixion. Nisan 14, 28 A.D.
    434 days + 4 days = 438 days

B. Nisan (Abib)17, 28 A.D. Crucifixion to Resurrection
    3 days

C. 7 sevens later Jesus baptizes the Disciples and others with the Holy Spirit and Fire at Pentecost, 49 days

    TOTAL   490 days, or 70 sevens.

D. 490 days from the Baptism of Jesus Christ, The Messiah, to the baptism of the Apostles with the Holy Spirit and fire at Pentecost.

The following scriptural calendar timing points in Jesus life set up the biblical framework for dating the specific events in the Ministry of the Messiah, Jesus Christ. Each timing point must line up or be explained.

(1.) The Messiah, had to start his ministry after Pontius Pilate was Governor of Judea according to Luke 3:1.which happened in 26 A.D..

(2.) The Ministry of Messiah, began in 26 A.D. to agree with John 2:20, about two months after his Baptism and at the Passover Feast. The Priests and Pharisees said, "What miraculous sign can you show us to prove your authority to do all this?" Jesus answered them, "Destroy this Temple and I will raise it again in three days" The Jews replied, "you are going to rebuild the Temple in three days and it has taken 46 years to build this Temple." But the Temple he had spoken of was his body. The Temple was started rebuilding in 19/20 BC making this year 27 AD

(3.) Luke 3:23 When all the people were being baptized. Jesus was baptized too....v23 Now Jesus himself was about thirty years old when he began his ministry. (Num 4:47 Priesthood started at 30) Baptism year 26 AD.

(4.) By Deduction the Birth of Jesus Christ must happen in 3/2 B.C. and agree with John 2:20 and Luke 3:23.

(5.) The ministry of Jesus, The Messiah, started in the 15th year of Tiberius Caesar. Tiberius took over in 11 B.C. but Augustus did not die until 14B.C. therefore the Ministry of Jesus Christ must start between 26 and 29 A.D.

(6.) The Passover Lamb must be a male lamb of the first year and therefore Jesus' crucifixion must happen in 28 A.D. before he is 31 years of age.

(7.) The Roman census or event commemorating Caesar Augustus 25th year and given a new title (3/2 B.C.). Luke 2 There is no record of a 3/2 BC census but many references to affirming the new title of Caesar as the Father of the Roman Empire (there were census in 8/7 BC and in 3/4 AD). This Roman Senate affirmation that Caesar Augustus is the Father of the Roman Empire would agree with the trip to Bethlehem for the birth of Jesus, This scenario allows The Messiah, Jesus Christ to be about 30 years old in 26 AD.

(8.) Herod's Death is in dispute and wont fit with the more reliable point of Jesus Christ starting his ministry at Age thirty (Josephus records Herod's death as 4 B.C.), but the eclipse mentioned when Herod murdered two Rabbi's is recorded as happening in 1B.C., and Herod's death was celebrated in Israel as Jan 10, 1B.C. And the timing of the building of the Temple lines up with Jesus being born in 3B.C. and Herod dying in 1 BC. Or possibly Luke could be referring to Herod's son.

(9.) Luke 2:1 Jesus was born when Quirinius was Governor of Syria. Quirinius (Cyrenius) was Governor 8/7 BC and 3/4 AD, but was over the registration of the approval of Senate Decree and the 750th anniversary of the founding of the Roman Empire. Oath of allegiance ordered to celebrate Augustus Caesar's silver jubilee on February 5, 2 BC. This would fit with Luke and with birth of Jesus Christ. This celebration marked the 25th anniversary of Augustus' elevation to supreme power by the Senate and people of Rome. It was also the 750th anniversary of the founding of Rome. At this celebration, the Senate conferred upon him the title "Pater Patriae" (Father of his Country).

The year before, Augustus sent out a decree requiring "the entire Roman people" throughout the empire to register their approval for the bestowal of this honor. This registration was required of all Roman citizens and others of distinguished rank among Rome's client kingdoms such as Judea. Cyrenius is Governor of Syria. Cyrenius came himself into Judea, which was now added to the province of Syria, to take an account of their substance. Josephus - Antiquities of the Jews - Book 18.

(10) Jesus must be born in Bethlehem, thirty years prior.

(11) The Anointed one must come into ministry on Rosh Hashanah the First Day of the Month, of the first month of the year in 27 AD to fulfill Daniel Prophecy.

Dating of the ministry of Jesus Christ must comply with all of these timing points

Full Transcription of Luke 3:1, 3:23 and John 2:20 and appropriate dates.

Luke's dating of the ministry of Jesus in Luke 3 and Gospel of John's reporting of Temple experience John 2:20 set the parameters for the most accurate dates for dating Jesus ministry and life.

Luke 3:1 In the fifteenth year of the reign of Tiberius Caesar (Tiberius took over in 11 AD which translates to 26AD but Caesar did not die until 14 AD which translates to 29 AD) when Pontius Pilate was Governor of Judea (A.D. 26-36), Herod was tetrarch of Galilee, his brother Phillip tetrarch of Iturea and Traconits and Lysanius tetrarch of Abilene. During the high priesthood of Annas and Caiaphas started in 26 AD.

Luke 3:23 When all the people were being baptized. Jesus was baptized too….v23 Now Jesus himself was about thirty years old when he began his ministry. (Num 4:47 Priesthood started at 30)

John 2:20, about two months after his Baptism and at the Passover Feast when Jesus cleansed the Temple. The Priests and Pharisees said, What miraculous sign can you show us to prove your authority to do all this? Jesus answered them, "Destroy this Temple and I will raise it again in three days" The Jews replied, "you are going to rebuild the Temple in Three days and it has taken 46 years to build this Temple." But the Temple he had spoken of was his body. (The Temple building was started in 19-20 BC timing confirms the year of this Passover as A.D. 27)

In conclusion, the scriptures line up with incredible specificity to set out dates, demands, and fulfillments on the life of Jesus Christ. There are more than three hundred fulfilled prophecies on the first coming of the Lord. Jesus fulfilled the spring Feasts of the Lord, the shadow picture of the Jewish wedding and the requirements of the Torah. In him who is our Savior and GOD, not some, but all, the Torah has been fulfilled by our Lord Jesus Christ for his first coming.

Fatal Errors in the present theology

The 360 day Prophetic year

The most significant failure of using an incorrect calendar is the decision by some Theologians to create the prophetic year of 360 days from an assumption they make from Genesis 8:4&5. These theologians tell you how to reconcile the 360 day calendar year back to the solar year. Then subtract that contrived number from Daniel 9 timing of 483 years to correct the error 5.25 days per year or 2,536 days or 7 plus years.

Doesn't it make more sense for GOD
    to tell Gabriel
    to tell Daniel 476 years.

Each of the theories that ignore the Sacred Calendar misses the incredible beauty of GOD's Prophetic fulfillments. Theologians settle for man made conclusions based on the calendars, cultures, and teachings that were well meaning but founded on an incorrect facts.

Daniel 9 Gabriel's words of prophecy to Daniel
Starting date for the decree to rebuild Jerusalem

Theologians with their man-made calendars, compound their error, when looking at Daniel 9, by using a incorrect starting point.

There are four commands to restore and rebuild Jerusalem:
1. Proclamation of Cyrus Ezra 1:1-4 in the year 536 BC

2. Order issued by Darius Ezra 6:1-12 in the year 516 BC
3. Decree issued by Artaxerxes I Ezra 7:12-26 year 457 BC
4. Letters from Artaxerxes I Nehemiah 2:7-8 year 444 BC

Theologians are trying to get the Bible to agree with our Christian Holidays and natural phenomena's. (Solar eclipses)

This is the timing needed to match their incorrect theory
1. Palm Sunday needs to agree with the Triumphal entry at the Passover Feast
2. Jesus needs to be crucified on a Friday on the fourteenth day of the month.
3. Daniel 9 needs a year when Friday is the First day of the month and is 483 years from the decree of some King in Babylon to send the Jews to rebuild Jerusalem.
4. The Sun was blotted out by a solar eclipse on March 19, 33AD and this is the day theologians need to be Passover
5. Three and one half year ministry of Jesus Christ
6. Resurrection is on Sunday, or the first day of the week, before dawn

If you use the contrived calendar trying to get to The eclipse in the year 33 when the fourteenth day of the month is a Friday, then the theologians use Nehemiah's appointment as Governor in the 20th year of King Artaxerxes 444 BC as the starting point for rebuilding Jerusalem. They are able to get to the year, but the totality of the timing requirements exposes many fatal errors.

The fatal errors to Jesus being crucified in 33 AD are on every facet.
1. Jesus is too old
2. Jesus ministry is over 7 years in length.
3. The eclipse is on a Sunday instead of Good Friday March 19, 33AD
4. Their date for Passover is Friday April 3, 33AD
5. The High Sabbath of Unleavened Bread is not part of their Feast days
6. There are 5 days instead of 4 from the Triumphal entry to Good Friday
7. No record of Jesus attending but four of the Appointed Feasts of GOD
8. The ministry start is not in the 15th year of the reign of Tiberius
9. Many more

GOD's prophecies aren't approximations: they are the word of GOD.

There are fatal errors in each one of these attempts to use a calendar other than the Sacred Calendar given by GOD and trying to date the prophecies of GOD with other calendars:
1. Jesus is wrong age (36 years old assuming 3/2 BC)
2. John 2:20 sets the Ministry start at year 26AD (Ministry Length 7 years)
3. Luke 3:23 Says Jesus is about 30 years of age when he started his ministry
4. The Solar eclipse March 19, 33AD is on a Sunday (not

Good Friday)

5. Passover is always followed by the High Sabbath of Unleavened Bread and not the weekly Sabbath, Friday can not be the day of Crucifixion and the triumphant entry be more than 4 days prior. It can't be on Palm Sunday!

6. Jesus, when he spoke to the Disciples in the upper room, told them he was in the tomb 3 days and 3 nights and raised on the third day. Good Friday to Easter Sunrise is just 36 hours. Looking backwards you cant say time was counted inclusively.

7. The starting date of 444 BC is the writing of the letters to Nehemiah for safe passage to Jerusalem and authority to get wood from the great forest, but not the decree to rebuild Jerusalem which came in first day of the first month 457 BC in Ezra 7.

And many more.

Notes:

Part Two

Introduction
Part Two

Proving the Prophet Daniel
Seventy week ministry of
Jesus Christ, The Messiah.

The following record details the Lord's movement day by day, the movements are enhanced with the Feasts of GOD and the years and months are calculated from Nasa calculations of the historical cycle of the moon over Jerusalem.

Notice there are no mentions of weeks, months, or years in the Gospels referring to Christ's movement, there is one reference to the harvest being four months away, but the reference is not detailing any movement or lengthy stay of the Lord, and last there is one reference to Jesus living in Capernaum, but again there is no indication referring to a period of time. In general, the Lord's movements are referred to in daily increments.

The schedule detail is divided into the following categories starting with Jesus Christ Baptism Shevat 19, 26 AD:
    The Ministry is divided into seventy weeks,
    The daily schedule is numbered from 1 day to 490 days,
    There are separate periodic details for the 40 days in the wilderness,

The months are based on the sighting of the renewed moon and are in Hebrew.

The daily record fits with all descriptions, prophecies, feast schedules, and scriptures. The record and the following chapters answer the these questions:
1. Why could Mary not touch Jesus after the resurrection?
2. If the anointed one was cut off in the midst of the 62 week, (according to Daniel 9) who was the anointed one and when was he anointed and when is the 62nd week if Jesus had a three and one half year ministry?
3. Where was Jesus Christ during the five Feasts of GOD not mentioned in the Bible if Jesus had a three and one half year ministry?
4. Do you think Jesus Christ was "not doing anything worth recording" during the nearly two years if Jesus ministry is three and one half years in length?
5. What is the proper date for the Anointed one coming in 483 years, mentioned in Daniel 9? What is the date of the beginning? Who anointed Jesus and Why was Jesus Baptized?
6. If Jesus was crucified on Friday, what year and what calendar are you using? Was Jesus using the same calendar? In what year is Passover (celebrated on the 14th day of the month) on the 14th day of the month and the 14th is a Friday or sixth day of the week and Friday is 4 days after Palm Sunday.

The Seventy Week Ministry
of Jesus Christ

Day of ministry	Day of the Week	Hebrew month and day	Location

Day-by-Day
Week-by-Week

Week One of the Seventy week Ministry of Jesus Christ, The Messiah

The Baptism and Anointing of The Messiah, Jesus Christ

Year 26 AD

1	1st day	Shevat 19	**Jordan River**

Mt. 3:13   Mk. 1:9-11   Lk. 3:21-22

Luke: Then Jesus came from Galilee to the Jordan to be baptized by John the Baptist. And when Jesus had been baptized, he at once, came up from the water, and suddenly the heavens opened and he saw the Spirit of God descending like a dove and coming down on him. And suddenly there was a voice from heaven, "This is my Son, the Beloved: my favor rest on him."

Matthew: Jesus came from Galilee to John at the Jordan to be baptized by him. John would have prevented him, saying, "I need to be baptized by you and do you come to me". But Jesus answered him, "Let it be so now for it is proper for us in this way to fulfill all righteousness".

Daniel 9:26: After the sixty two sevens the Anointed one will be cut off and will have nothing. This date is the start date for the 62 sevens.

2	2nd day	Shevat 20	**Wilderness Day 1**

Mt. 4:1-11   Mk. 1:12-13   Lk. 4:1-13

Then Jesus was led by the Spirit into the wilderness to fast for forty days.

| 3 | 3rd day | Shevat 21 | **Wilderness Day 2** |

After the Lord's Baptism

Luke: Now Jesus himself was about thirty years old when he began his Ministry

4	4th day	Shevat 22	**Wilderness Day 3**
5	5th day	Shevat 23	**Wilderness Day 4**
6	6th day	Shevat 24	**Wilderness Day 5**
7	Sabbath	Shevat 25	**Wilderness Day 6**

Week Two
Year 26 AD

Then Jesus was led by the Spirit into the wilderness to fast for forty days

8	1st day	Shevat 26	**Wilderness Day 7**
9	2nd day	Shevat 27	**Wilderness Day 8**
10	3rd day	Shevat 28	**Wilderness Day 9**
11	4th day	Shevat 29	**Wilderness Day 10**
12	5th day	Adar 01	**Wilderness Day 11**
13	6th day	Adar 02	**Wilderness Day 12**
14	Sabbath	Adar 03	**Wilderness Day 13**

Week Three
Year 26 AD

Then Jesus was led by the Spirit into the wilderness to fast for forty days.

15	1st day	Adar 04	**Wilderness Day 14**
16	2nd day	Adar 05	**Wilderness Day 15**
17	3rd day	Adar 06	**Wilderness Day 16**
18	4th day	Adar 07	**Wilderness Day 17**
19	5th day	Adar 08	**Wilderness Day 18**
20	6th day	Adar 09	**Wilderness Day 19**
21	Sabbath	Adar 10	**Wilderness Day 20**

Week Four
Year 26 AD

Jesus was led by the Spirit into the wilderness to fast for forty days.

22	1st day	Adar 11	**Wilderness Day 21**
23	2nd day	Adar 12	**Wilderness Day 22**
24	3rd day	Adar 13	**Wilderness Day 23**
25	4th day	Adar 14	**Wilderness Day 24**

Feast of Purim, one month before Passover celebrating God's mighty deliverance of Mordecai and Esther.

26	5th day	Adar 15	**Wilderness Day 25**
27	6th day	Adar 16	**Wilderness Day 26**
28	Sabbath	Adar 17	**Wilderness Day 27**

Week Five
Year 26 AD

Jesus was led by the Spirit into the wilderness to fast for forty days.

29	1st day	Adar 18	**Wilderness Day 28**
30	2nd day	Adar 19	**Wilderness Day 29**
31	3rd day	Adar 20	**Wilderness Day 30**
32	4th day	Adar 21	**Wilderness Day 31**
33	5th day	Adar 22	**Wilderness Day 32**
34	6th day	Adar 23	**Wilderness Day 33**
35	Sabbath	Adar 24	**Wilderness Day 34**

Week Six
Year 26 AD

Jesus was led by the Spirit into the wilderness to fast for forty days.

| 36 | 1st day | Adar 25 | **Wilderness Day 35** |
| 37 | 2nd day | Adar 26 | **Wilderness Day 36** |

38	3rd day	Adar 27	**Wilderness Day 37**
39	4th day	Adar 28	**Wilderness Day 38**
40	5th day	Adar 29	**Wilderness Day 39**

Mt. 4:1-13

Matthew 4:1-13: The tempter said to him "If you are the Son of GOD, tell these stones to turn into loaves" But Jesus said "It is written man does not live on bread alone, but on every word that comes from mouth of GOD."

The devil then took Jesus to Jerusalem and set him on the parapet of the Temple. If you are the Son of GOD, he said, throw yourself down for scripture says, "He has given his angels about you and they will carry you in their arms in case you trip over a stone" Jesus said to him, "It is written, do not put the Lord your GOD to the test."

Next, taking him to a very high mountain, the devil showed him all the kingdoms of the world and their splendor. And he said to Jesus, "I will give you all of these, if you will fall at my feet and do me homage" Then Jesus replied, "It is written, The Lord your GOD is the one you must do homage, him alone you must serve."

(John 1:19-25) Jerusalem sent Pharisees to question John the Baptist (Many days after baptism). John the Baptist being questioned by Pharisees and Levites from Jerusalem, "Are you the Christ, Are you Elijah?
    then John replied, I am not.

Are you the Prophet? I am not.
Who are you?
We must take back an answer to those who sent us.
John's reply, I am as Isaiah prophesied:
A voice of one that cries in the desert: prepare a way for the Lord, Make his paths straight.

The beginning of the New Year according to the Sacred Calendar

The renewed moon is 3% illuminated and 14 degrees in the horizon.

27 AD Rosh Hashanah, The exact day 483 years after Ezra left to rebuild Jerusalem, and fulfilling the prophecy in Daniel 9.

| 41 | 6th day | Nisan 01 | **Wilderness Day 40** |

John1:29-34 The next day, John saw Jesus, The Messiah, coming towards him and said,

"Look! there is the lamb of GOD, that takes away the sin of the world. It was of him that I said, "behind me comes one who has passed ahead of me because he existed before me. I did not know him myself, and yet my purpose in coming was to baptize with water was so that he might be revealed to Israel". And John said, "I saw the Spirit come down on him like a dove from heaven and rest on him …v33 The man on whom you see the Spirit come down and rest is the one who is to baptize with the Holy Spirit. I have seen and I testify that he is the Chosen One of GOD."

| 42 | Sabbath | Nisan 02 | **Bethany E. of Jordan** |

Jn. 1:35-39

John: The next day as John stood there again with two of his disciples, Jesus went past and John looked towards him and said, "Look, there is the lamb of GOD" and the two disciples followed him….

Week Seven of the Seventy week Ministry of Jesus Christ, The Messiah
Year 27 AD

| 43 | 1st day | Nisan 03 | **Bethany E of Jordan** |

John1:43-47: The next day, after Jesus had decided to leave for Galilee, he met Phillip and said "Follow me"…Phillip found Nathaniel and said to him. "We have found him of whom Moses spoke in the Law and the Prophets".

44	2nd day	Nisan 04	**Going to Cana**
45	3rd day	Nisan 05	**Going to Cana**
46	4th day	Nisan 06	**Cana**

John 2:1-11: On the third day there was a wedding at Cana in Galilee. Jesus first miracle is the turning of the water to wine.

| 47 | 5th day | Nisan 07 | **To Capernaum** |

First Disciples follow Jesus

Matthew 4:18-22: As he was walking by the Sea of

Galilee he saw Simon and Andrew
"Come follow me and I will make you fishers of men"
After preaching, Jesus said, " Put out into the deep water and let down the nets for a catch" They caught fish until the nets were breaking, so they pulled up their boats on shore, left everything, and followed him.

48	6th day	Nisan 08	**Capernaum**
49	Sabbath	Nisan 09	**Capernaum**

Mt. 8:14-17   Mk. 1:21-34   Lk. 4:31-41

Delivered the man with evil spirit in the Temple
Matthew: Jesus was Teaching in the Synagogue as was his custom, there was a man with a demon spirit and he cried out at the top of his voice "Ha, what do you want with us, Jesus of Nazareth?" Jesus said, "Be quiet…Come out of him"…What is this teaching with authority and power, he gives orders to evil spirits and they come out.

Jesus healed Peter's Mother in Law
Jesus left the Synagogue and went to Simon Peter's house. Now Simon's mother in law was suffering from a high fever…So He rebuked the fever and it left her and she got up, at once, and served them.

When it was almost time for Passover, Jesus went up to Jerusalem (John 2:12-13)
(This was probably a three to four day walk.)

The Seventy-Week Ministry, 73

Early ministry and
First trip to Jerusalem for the
Feast of Passover, Unleavened Bread, and First Fruits.

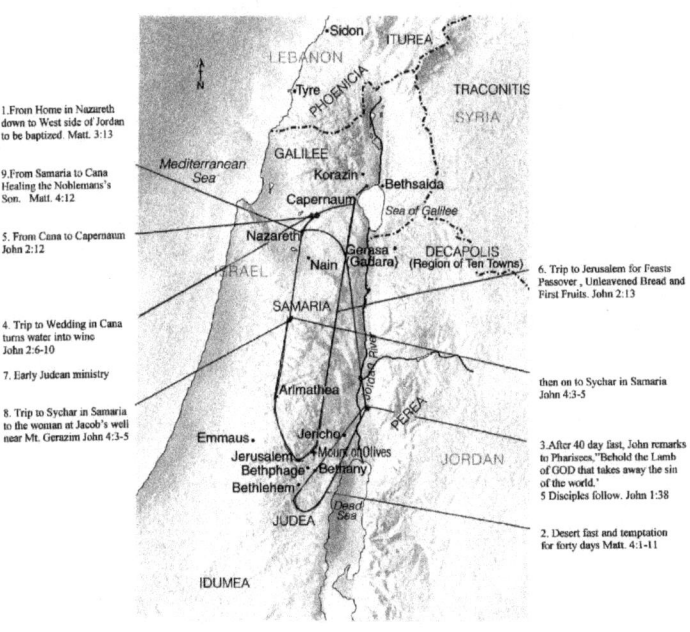

1. From Home in Nazareth down to West side of Jordan to be baptized. Matt. 3:13

9. From Samaria to Cana Healing the Nobleman's Son. Matt. 4:12

5. From Cana to Capernaum John 2:12

4. Trip to Wedding in Cana turns water into wine John 2:6-10

7. Early Judean ministry

8. Trip to Sychar in Samaria to the woman at Jacob's well near Mt. Gerazim John 4:3-5

6. Trip to Jerusalem for Feasts Passover, Unleavened Bread and First Fruits. John 2:13

then on to Sychar in Samaria John 4:3-5

3. After 40 day fast, John remarks to Pharisees, "Behold the Lamb of GOD that takes away the sin of the world."
5 Disciples follow. John 1:38

2. Desert fast and temptation for forty days Matt. 4:1-11

Week Eight
Year 27 AD

Passover
(Exodus 12:2-14)
The Feast of Unleavened Bread
(Exodus 12:15-18 and Leviticus 23:6-8)
First Fruits and its offering
(Leviticus 23:9-14)

| 50 | 1st day | Nisan 10 | **To Jerusalem** |

Jn. 2:12

John:: After this he went down to Capernaum with his Mother and brothers for a few days

Feast schedule: Preparation Day 1
The day the Passover Lamb is chosen and paraded through Jerusalem

| 51 | 6th day | Nisan 11 | **To Jerusalem** |

Feast schedule: Preparation Day 2
Preparation day for cleaning the house & preparing the family.

| 52 | 3rd day | Nisan 12 | **Jerusalem** |

Jn. 2:14-25

Jesus, The Messiah, cleanses the Temple

John: In the Temple courts he (Jesus) found men selling cattle, sheep, and doves, and others sitting at tables exchanging money. So Jesus made a whip out of cords and drove all from the temple area.... vs16 To those who sold doves Jesus said," Get these out of here! How dare you

turn my Father's House into a market."
Feast schedule:
Preparation day for cleaning and preparing the family Passover Lamb.

| 53 | 4th day | Nisan 13 | **Jerusalem** |

Jn. 2:23-25

Many saw, heard, and believed in Jesus, The Messiah.
John: Now while he was in Jerusalem at the Passover Feast, many people saw the miraculous signs he was doing and believed in his name.

Feast schedule:
Preparation day all leaven must be burned and meal preparation started.

| 54 | 5th day | Nisan 14 | **Jerusalem** |

Jn. 2:19-20

The Feast of Passover
Prophecy of resurrection by Jesus, by himself
John: Then the Jews demanded of him, what miraculous sign can you show us to prove your authority to do all this? Jesus answered them, "Destroy this temple and I will raise it up in three days."

Feast schedule:
Passover Lamb is sacrificed, roasted and eaten with bitter herbs.

| 55 | 6th day | Nisan 15 | **Jerusalem** |

The Feast of Unleavened Bread
Feast schedule:
High Sabbath of Unleavened Bread

| 56 | Sabbath | Nisan 16 | **Jerusalem** |

Weekly Sabbath

Week Nine
Year 27 AD
First Fruits and its offering

| 57 | 1st day | Nisan 17 | **Jerusalem** |

Jn. 3:1-21

Jesus tells Nicodemus, "You must be born again."
John: Now there was a man of the Pharisees named Nicodemus, a member of the Jewish ruling council. He came to Jesus at night and said, "Rabbi, we know you are a teacher who has come from GOD, For no one could perform the miraculous signs you are doing if GOD were not with him." In reply Jesus declared, "I tell you the truth, no one can enter the kingdom of GOD unless he is born again."

Feast schedule:
First Fruits wave offering of barley to the Lord

| 58 | 2nd day | Nisan 18 | **Jerusalem** |

Feast schedule: fourth day of The Feast of Unleavened Bread

| 59 | 3rd day | Nisan 19 | **Jerusalem** |

Feast schedule: fifth day of The Feast of Unleavened Bread

| 60 | 4th day | Nisan 20 | **Jerusalem** |

Feast schedule: sixth day of Feast of Unleavened Bread and preparation day for the High Sabbath.

| 61 | 5th day | Nisan 21 | **Jerusalem** |

Feast schedule: High Sabbath to end Unleavened Bread and First Fruits Feast of Yahweh

| 62 | 6th Day | Nisan 22 | **Jerusalem** |
| 63 | Sabbath | Nisan 23 | **Jerusalem** |

Week Ten
Year 27 AD

| 64 | 1st day | Nisan 24 | **Aenon near Salim** |

John 4:1: The Pharisees heard that Jesus was gaining and baptizing more disciples than John the Baptist, although in fact it was not Jesus who baptizes but his disciples. This is important because as Luke's Gospel 3:16 John baptized with water but the One who comes after John will baptize with the Holy Spirit and with Life.

| 65 | 2nd day | Nisan 25 | **Herod in Jerusalem** |

John the Baptist put in jail

Luke 3:19-20: But when John the Baptist rebuked Herod, the tetrarch, because of Herodias, his brother's wife and all the other evil things he had done. Herod added this to them all. He locked up John in prison.

| 66 | 3rd day | Nisan 26 | **Going to Galilee** |

Jn 4:4

| 67 | 4th day | Nisan 27 | **Jacob's Well** |

Jn 4:7-26

John 4:6-7: Now Jesus had to go through Samaria, so he came to a town named Sychar…..vs.6 Jacob's well was there and Jesus was tired from the journey and sat down by the well, It was about the sixth hour.

Woman at the well

John: When a Samaritan woman came to draw water: Jesus said to her, "Will you give me a drink?" The Samaritan woman said to him, "you are a Jew and I am a Samaritan woman. How can you ask me for a drink?" Jesus answered her, " If you knew the gift of GOD, and who it is, that asks you for a drink, you would have ask him and he would have given you living water."…. Jesus answered, "Everyone who drinks this water will thirst again, but whosoever drinks the water I give him will never thirst again, indeed the water I give him will become in him a spring of water welling up to eternal life."

| 68 | 5th day | Nisan 28 | **Sychar, Samaria** |

Jn 4:27-42

Many Samaritans believe

John: The woman put down her water pot and hurried back to town to tell the people, "come and see a man who has told me everything I have done. Could this be the Christ?" … Jesus speaking to the disciples "well I tell you, look around you, look at the fields, already they are white ready for the harvest. The Samaritan's said to the woman, "We no longer believe just because of what you said: now we have heard for ourselves, and we know that this man really is the Savior of the world."

69	6th Day	Nisan 29	**Leaving Nazareth**
70	Sabbath	Iyyar 01	**Resting**

Week Eleven
Year 27 AD

71	1st day	Iyyar 01	**Leaving Nazareth**

Mt. 4:12-16   Mk. 1:14-15   Lk. 4:14-15   Jn. 4:43-45

Jesus fulfills another prophecy

Matthew: When Jesus heard that John had been put in prison, he returned to Galilee, Leaving Nazareth, he went and lived in Capernaum, which was by the lake in the area of Zebulon and Napthali to fulfill what was said through the prophet Isaiah, "Land of Zebulon and land of Napthali, the way to the sea, along the Jordan, Galilee of the gentiles vs. 16 The people living in darkness have seen a great light: on those living in the land of the shadow of death a light has dawned." Again in Cana

72	2nd day	Iyyar 02	**Capernaum**

Jn 4:46-54

Jesus heals Royal official's son in another town.

John: And there was a certain royal official whose son lay sick at Capernaum....He went to Jesus and begged him to come and heal his son, who was close to death. ...Jesus said, "You may go, your son will live" The next day the official's servant confirmed his son was healed at the same hour as Jesus had spoken.

73	3rd Day	Iyyar 03	**Capernaum**
74	4th Day	Iyyar 04	**Capernaum**
75	5th Day	Iyyar 05	**Capernaum**
76	6th Day	Iyyar 06	**Capernaum**
77	Sabbath	Iyyar 07	**Capernaum**

Mk 1:21-28   Lk. 4:33-37

Mark: . . . and on the Sabbath (Jesus) began to teach the people, They were amazed at his teaching, because his message had authority.

Week Twelve
Year 27 AD

78	1st day	Iyyar 08	**Galilee**

Mt 4:12-17   Mk 1:14-15   Lk 4:14-15   Jn 4:43-45
And he preached throughout Galilee in their synagogues

79	2nd day	Iyyar 09	**Galilee**

Cities and towns in Galilee in Jesus time.

80	3rd Day	Iyyar 10	**Hazor, Chorazim**
81	4th Day	Iyyar 11	**Genneserat**
82	5th Day	Iyyar 12	**Magdala, Tiberius**
83	6th Day	Iyyar 13	**Cana, Nain**

| 84 | Sabbath | Iyyar 14 | **Galilee** |

Week Thirteen
Year 27 AD

| 85 | 1st day | Iyyar 15 | **Sea of Galilee** |

Mt 4:18-22   Mk 1:16-20

Matthew: One day as Jesus was standing by the Lake Genneserat, with the people crowded about, and listening to the word of God, he saw at the waters edge two boats, left there by the fishermen, who were cleaning their nets. Jesus got into one of the boats, the one belonging to Simon, and asked him to put out a little from the shore, and then he sat down and taught the people from the boat.

(Jesus rewards Simon for the use of his boat as a pulpit, with a giant catch of fish. After borrowing Simon's, later called Peter's, boat, Jesus sent him back to the sea for the largest catch of fish he had ever caught and it took two boats to bring in the fish. There were probably enough fish to pay off any debts the fishermen had and provide for the fishermen's family because it says they left everything and followed Jesus.)

| 86 | 2nd Day | Iyyar 16 | **Lake Genneserat** |
| 87 | 3rd Day | Iyyar 17 | **Around Galilee** |

Mt 4:23-25   Mk 1:35-39

Matthew: And Jesus went throughout Galilee teaching in their synagogues, preaching the good news of the kingdom and healing all their diseases. Vs 25 Large crowds followed from Galilee, Decapolis, Jerusalem, Judea and the region across the Jordan followed him.

88	4th Day	Iyyar 18	**Around Galilee**
89	5th Day	Iyyar 19	**Around Galilee**
90	6th Day	Iyyar 20	**Capernaum**

Mk 1:21-24   Lk 4:31-37

Mark: They went to Capernaum, and when the Sabbath came Jesus went into the synagogue and began to teach with great authority.

| 91 | Sabbath | Iyyar 21 | **Capernaum** |

Mk 1:24-28   Lk 4:33-38

Jesus delivers demon possessed man

Luke: In the synagogue there was a man possessed by a demon, an evil spirit. ...Vs. 34 "Be quiet, Come out of him", Jesus said sternly. ...Vs. 36 All the people were amazed and said to each other, What is this teaching with authority and power, he gives orders to the evil spirits and they come out.

Mt 8:14-17   Mk 1:29-34   Lk 4:38-41

Later on the Sabbath, Jesus healed Simon Peter's Mother-in-law and she got up and fixed dinner.

Week Fourteen
Year 27 AD

| 92 | 1st day | Iyyar 22 | **Mountainside** |

Mt 8:1-4   Mk 1:40-45   Lk 5:12-16
When he came down from the mountainside, large crowds followed him

| 93 | 2nd day | Iyyar 23 | **Near Capernaum** |

Jesus heals a man of leprosy

Matthew: A man with leprosy came and knelt before him and said "Lord If you are willing you can make me clean". Jesus reached out his hand and touched the man "I am willing, Be Clean" he said Then Jesus said "See that you don't tell anyone, but go show yourself to the priest and offer the gift Moses commanded as a testimony to them".

| 94 | 3rd day | Iyyar 24 | **Capernaum** |

Mt 9:1-8   Mk 2:1-12   Lk 5:17-26

Jesus heals the paralytic man

Luke: One day as he was teaching, Pharisees and teachers of the law, who had come from every village of Galilee and from Judea and Jerusalem were sitting there. And the power of the Lord was present for him to heal the sick. Some men brought a paralytic on a mat... When Jesus saw there faith he said, "Friend your sins are forgiven" .... To the Pharisees, "Why are you thinking these things in your hearts? Which is easier to say your sins are forgiven or get up and walk."

| 95 | 4th day | Iyyar 25 | **Lake Genneserat** |

Mt 9:9-13   Mk 2:13-17   Lk 5:27-32

Mark: Once again as Jesus went out beside the lake, a large crowd came to him and he began to teach them.

The Seventy-Week Ministry, 84

Short trips from Capernaum and Second trip to Jerusalem For the Feast of Shavuots (Pentecost)

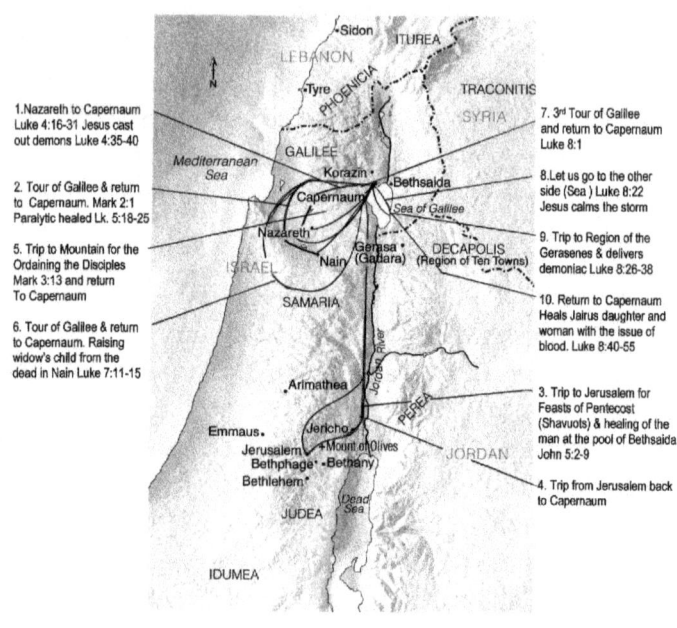

1. Nazareth to Capernaum Luke 4:16-31 Jesus cast out demons Luke 4:35-40

2. Tour of Galilee & return to Capernaum. Mark 2:1 Paralytic healed Lk. 5:18-25

5. Trip to Mountain for the Ordaining the Disciples Mark 3:13 and return To Capernaum

6. Tour of Galilee & return to Capernaum. Raising widow's child from the dead in Nain Luke 7:11-15

7. 3rd Tour of Galilee and return to Capernaum Luke 8:1

8. Let us go to the other side (Sea) Luke 8:22 Jesus calms the storm

9. Trip to Region of the Gerasenes & delivers demoniac Luke 8:26-38

10. Return to Capernaum Heals Jairus daughter and woman with the issue of blood. Luke 8:40-55

3. Trip to Jerusalem for Feasts of Pentecost (Shavuots) & healing of the man at the pool of Bethsaida John 5:2-9

4. Trip from Jerusalem back to Capernaum

Jesus calls Matthew, formerly known as Levi

As he walked along. He saw Levi, son of Alphaeus, sitting at the tax collectors booth, "Follow me" Jesus said and Levi got up and followed him. Later he had dinner at Levi's house.

96	5th Day	Iyyar 26	**To Jerusalem**
97	6th Day	Iyyar 27	**To Jerusalem**
98	Sabbath	Iyyar 28	**To Jerusalem**

Week Fifteen
Year 27 AD

99	1st day	Iyyar 29	**To Jerusalem**

Jn 5:1

John: Some time later, Jesus went up to Jerusalem for a Feast of the Jews.

("Feast of the Jews" is a very incomplete translation, without any deference to the information in the Torah or Old Testament. The Feasts are the Lord's appointed times to meet with his people in the place where Yahweh shall place his name.)

100	2nd Day	Sivan 01	**To Jerusalem**
101	3rd Day	Sivan 02	**To Jerusalem**
102	4th Day	Sivan 03	**To Jerusalem**
103	5th Day	Sivan 04	**To Jerusalem**

| 104 | 6th Day | Sivan 05 | **To Jerusalem** |
| 105 | Sabbath | Sivan 06 | **Jerusalem** |

5:2
First Day of Yahweh's Feast of Shavuots
(Pentecost)
Leviticus 23:15-22

Jesus heals invalid at pool of Bethesada
John: Now there is in Jerusalem, near the Sheep Gate, a pool, which in Aramaic is called Bethesada and which is surrounded by five covered colonnades. ...Vs5 One who was there had been an invalid for thirty-eight years. When Jesus saw him lying there and learned that he had been in this condition for a long time, Jesus asked him "Do you want to get well?" ...Vs7 Then Jesus said "Get up! Pick up your matt and walk."

The day on which this took place was a Sabbath and so the Jews said to the man who had been healed. "It is the Sabbath: the law forbids you to carry your matt."

Week Sixteen
Year 27 AD
Pentecost, The Feast of the Yahweh
Centered around the wheat harvest.
It is a required attendance for all males over the age of thirteen to meet with their GOD in Jerusalem.

| 106 | 1st day | Sivan 07 | **High Sabbath** |

Leviticus 23:15-16 (Counting the weeks and the Omer) And ye shall count unto you from the morrow after the Sabbath from the day that ye brought the sheaf of the wave offering (offering at First Fruits): seven Sabbaths shall be complete: Seven unto the morrow after the seventh Sabbath shall ye number fifty days: and ye shall offer a new meat offering unto Yahweh.

Feast schedule:

High Sabbath of the Feast of Pentecost (Shavuots) This feast is centered around the wheat harvest. Both verse John 5:9-10 in the Greek show there is "a" Sabbath and a "The" Sabbath. It repeats this order in John 5:16.

| 107 | 2nd day | Sivan 08 | **Jerusalem** |

Jn 5:16

Feast Schedule: Day three

Jesus persecuted for healing on the Sabbath

John: So, because Jesus was doing these (miraculous) things on "a" Sabbath, the Jews persecuted him. Jesus said to them, "My Father is always at his work, to this very day and I too am working." For this reason, the Jews tried harder to kill him. Not only was he breaking "The" Sabbath, but he was even calling GOD his own Father, making himself equal with GOD.

| 108 | 3rd day | Sivan 09 | **Jerusalem** |

Feast schedule: day four

109	4th day	Sivan 10	**Jerusalem**
Feast schedule: day five			
110	5th day	Sivan 11	**Jerusalem**
Feast schedule: day six			
111	6th day	Sivan 12	**Jerusalem**
Feast schedule: day seven			
112	Sabbath	Sivan 13	**Jerusalem**

Week Seventeen
Year 27 AD

113	1st Day	Sivan 14	**Withdrawal to Sea**
114	2nd Day	Sivan 15	**Withdrawal to Sea**
115	3rd Day	Sivan 16	**Withdrawal to Sea**
116	4th Day	Sivan 17	**Withdrawal to Sea**
117	5th Day	Sivan 18	**Withdrawal to Sea**
118	6th Day	Sivan 19	**Galilee**

Mt 9:14-17   Mk 2:18-22   Lk 5:33-39

Pharisees question Jesus about fasting

Mark: Now John's disciples and the Pharisees were fasting. ...How is it that John's disciples and the disciples of the Pharisees are fasting, but yours are not?

Jesus answered, "How can the guests of the bridegroom fast while he is with them? They cannot, so long as they have him with them. But the time will come when the bridegroom will be taken from them, and on that day they shall fast."

| 119 | Sabbath | Sivan 20 | **Galilee** |

Mt 12:1-8   Mk 2:23-28   Lk 6:1-5

Jesus questioned about disciples picking grain on the Sabbath

Luke: One Sabbath, Jesus was going through the grain fields, and his disciples began to pick some heads of grain, rub them in their hands and eat the kernels. Some of the Pharisees asked why are you doing what is unlawful on the Sabbath. Jesus answered them, "Have you not read what David did when he and his companions were hungry? He entered the House of GOD and took the consecrated bread, he ate what is lawful only the priests to eat. And he also gave some to his companions." Then Jesus said to them, " The Son of Man is Lord of the Sabbath".

Mt 12:9-14   Mk 3:1-6   Lk 6:6-11

Jesus asked, is it lawful to heal on the Sabbath?

Matthew: Going from that place, he went into their synagogue, and a man with a shriveled hand was there. Looking for a reason to accuse Jesus, they asked him is it lawful to heal on the Sabbath.

Jesus said to them, "If any of you has a sheep that falls in a pit, on the Sabbath will you not take hold of it and lift it out? How much more valuable is a man than a sheep.

Therefore it is lawful to do good on the Sabbath. Stretch out your hand!" So he stretched it out and it was completely restored, ...vs. 14 but the Pharisees went out and plotted how they might kill Jesus.

Week Eighteen
Year 27 AD

| 120 | 1st day | Sivan 21 | **Sea of Galilee** |

Mt 12:15-16   Mk 3:7-12   Lk 6:12-16

Mark: Jesus withdrew, with his disciples, to the lake and a large crowd from Galilee followed, ...vs10 for he had healed so many.

The crowd was so large and Jesus and the Disciples, left in a boat to escape the crush of the crowd.

| 121 | 2nd day | Sivan 22 | **Mountainside** |

Mt 10:2-4   Mk 3:13-19   Lk 6:14-16

The appointing of the twelve Apostles

Mark: Jesus went up on a mountainside and called to him those he wanted and they came to him. Jesus appointed twelve, designating them Apostles. That they might be with him and that he might send them out to preach and to have authority to drive out demons.

| 122 | 3rd Day | Sivan 23 | **Capernaum** |
| 123 | 4th Day | Sivan 24 | **Capernaum** |

Mt 11:1

Matthew: After Jesus had finished instructing his twelve disciples, he went on from there to teach and preach in the towns of Galilee.

| 124 | 5th day | Sivan 25 | **Capernaum** |

Mt 11:2-6   Lk 7:18-35

John the Baptist sends disciples to ask if Jesus is the Christ?

Matthew: When John heard in prison what Christ was doing, he sent his disciples to ask him, "Are you the one who was to come or should we look for another?" Jesus replied, "Go back and report to John what you hear and see: The blind receive sight, the lame walk, those who have leprosy are cured, the deaf hear, the dead are raised, and the good news is preached to the poor."

| 125 | 6th day | Sivan 26 | **Tour of Galilee** |

Mt 11:20-24   Lk 10:13-15

Woe to the cities that don't repent.

Matthew: Then Jesus began to denounce the cities in which most of his miracles had been performed, because they did not repent.

(Probably, these towns did not welcome the disciples because of their hard hearts.)

Vs. 21 Woe to you Korazin! Woe to you Bethsaida! If the miracles that were performed in you had been performed in Tyre and Sidon they would have repented in sackcloth and ashes.

| 126 | Sabbath | Sivan 27 | **Tour of Galilee** |

Mt 11:25-27   Lk 10:21-22

Jesus confirms that his yoke is easy and his burden is light

Matthew: Come to me, all you who are weary and burdened and I will give you rest. Take my yoke upon you and learn from me, for I am gentle and humble in heart and you will find rest for the your souls. For my yoke is easy and my burden is light.

Week Nineteen
Year 27 AD

| 127 | 1ˢᵗ day | Sivan 28 | **Tour of Galilee** |

Lk 7:36-50
Jesus eating at a Pharisee's house

Luke: Now one of the Pharisees invited Jesus to have dinner with him, so he went to the Pharisees house and reclined at the table. When a woman, who had lived a sinful life, in the town learned that Jesus was eating at the Pharisees house. She brought in an alabaster jar of perfume and as she stood behind at his feet weeping, She began to wet his feet with her tears. Then she wiped them with her hair kissed them and poured perfume on them.

| 128 | 2ⁿᵈ day | Sivan 29 | **Tour of Galilee** |

Lk 8:1-3
Women supporting Jesus out of their own means

Luke: After this, Jesus traveled from one town and village to another proclaiming the good news of the kingdom of GOD. The twelve were with him and also some women who had been cured of evil spirits and diseases: Mary

Magdalene, from whom seven demons had come out: Joanna the wife of Cuza, the manager of Herod's household: Susanna and many others. These women were helping to support them out of their own means.

| 129 | 3rd day | Sivan 30 | **Tour of Galilee** |

Mt 12:22-37   Mk 3:20-30

Jesus delivers the demon-possessed man who was blind and mute.

Matthew: Then they brought him a demon-possessed man who was blind and mute and Jesus healed him, so that he could both talk and see. All the people were astonished and said, "Could this be the Son of David?" But the Pharisees heard this, they said, "it is only by Beelzebub, the prince of demons, that this fellow drives out demons." Jesus knew their thoughts and said to them, "Every kingdom divided against itself will be ruined, ... If Satan drives out Satan, he is divided against himself.... vs. 27 And if I drive out demons by Beelzebub by whom do your people drive them out? .... Vs. 28 but if I drive out demons by the Spirit of GOD, then the Kingdom of GOD has come upon you."

| 130 | 4th day | Tammuz 01 | **Tour of Galilee** |

Mt 12:38-48   Mk 3:20-30

Pharisees asking for a miraculous sign

Matthew: Then some of the Pharisees and teachers of the law said to him, "Teacher, we want to see a miraculous sign from you." Jesus answered, A wicked and adulterous generation asks for a miraculous sign, but none will be given except the sign of the prophet Jonah. For as the prophet Jonah was three days and three nights in the belly of a huge fish, so the Son of Man will be three days and three nights in the heart of the earth."

131	5th Day	Tammuz 02	**Tour of Galilee**
132	6th Day	Tammuz 03	**Tour of Galilee**
133	Sabbath	Tammuz 04	**Tour of Galilee**

Week Twenty
Year 27 AD

134	1st Day	Tammuz 05	**Tour of Galilee**
135	2nd Day	Tammuz 06	**Tour of Galilee**

Mt 12:46-50   Mk 3:31-35   Lk 8:19-21

Jesus' Mother and brothers come to visit.

Luke: Someone told him, "Your mother and brothers are standing outside wanting to see you" Jesus replied, "My Mother and brothers are those who hear GOD's word and put it into practice"

Matthew 13:1 That same day Jesus went out of the house and sat by the lake.

136	3rd Day	Tammuz 07	**Sea of Galilee**
137	4th Day	Tammuz 08	**Sea of Galilee**
138	5th Day	Tammuz 09	**Sea of Galilee**

Mt 13:1-19   Mk 4:1-9   Lk 8:4-8

Matthew: Such crowds gathered around him that Jesus got into a boat and sat in it, while all the people stood on

the shore. Then he told them parables:
> **Parable of the Sower and its explanation**
> **Parable of growing seed**
> **Parable of the weeds**
> **Parable of the mustard seed, yeast, hidden treasure, pearl merchant, and fish net.**

Matthew 13-53: When Jesus had finished these parables, he moved on from there, Coming to his hometown. (Nazareth)

| 139 | 6th Day | Tammuz 10 | **Nazareth** |
| 140 | Sabbath | Tammuz 11 | **Nazareth** |

Mt 13:54-43   Mk 6:1-6

Prophet is without honor in his hometown

Matthew: Jesus began teaching the people in their synagogue and they were amazed. "Where did this man get this wisdom and these miraculous powers?" Isn't this the carpenter's son? .... But Jesus said to them, "Only in his hometown and in his own house is a prophet without honor."

Week Twenty-One
Year 27 AD

| 141 | 1st Day | Tammuz 12 | **Capernaum** |
| 142 | 2nd Day | Tammuz 13 | **Crossing Sea** |

Mt 8:23-27   Mk 4:35-41   Lk 8:22-25

Jesus calms the storm

Mark: That day when evening came, Jesus said to his

disciples, "Let us go over to the other side" Leaving the crowd behind, they took him along, just as he was, in the boat. There were other boats with them. A furious squall came up. ...Teacher don't you care that we drown? Jesus got up, rebuked the wind and said to the waves, "Quiet, be still." ... Vs. 40 He said to the disciples, "Why are you afraid? Do you still have no faith?"

Vs 41 They were terrified and asked each other, "Who is this? Even the wind and the waves obey him!"

143	3rd Day	Tammuz 14	**Gadarenes**
144	4th Day	Tammuz 15	**Gadarenes**
145	5th Day	Tammuz 16	**Gadarenes**

Mt 8:28-33   Mk 5:1-20   Lk 8:26-37

Jesus delivers two men and sends demons into herd of pigs.

Matthew: When Jesus arrived at the other side in the region of the Gadarenes: two demon-possessed men coming from the tombs met him. They were so violent that no one could pass that way. Demons speaking, "What do you want with us Son of GOD? Have you come here to torture us before the appointed time? Note: Jesus called them out of the men and they went into a herd of pigs who rushed over a cliff.... vs. 34 Then the whole town went out to meet Jesus. And when they saw him, they asked him to leave their region.

(Note: These pigs were raised for the sacrifices to the temple of Zeus.)

| 146 | 6th Day | Tammuz 17 | **Decapolis** |
| 147 | Sabbath | Tammuz 18 | **Decapolis** |

Week Twenty-Two
Year 27 AD

| 148 | 1st Day | Tammuz 19 | **Decapolis** |
| 149 | 2nd Day | Tammuz 20 | **Decapolis** |

Lk 8:38-39

Jesus sends man delivered of demons to be a witness in his home town

Luke: The man from whom the demons had gone out, begged to go with him, but Jesus sent him away saying, "Return home and tell how much GOD has done for you."

So the man went away and told all over town how much Jesus had done for him.

150	3rd Day	Tammuz 21	**Decapolis**
151	4th Day	Tammuz 22	**Decapolis**
152	5th Day	Tammuz 23	**Crossing Sea**

Mt 9:1-8 Mk 2:3-12 Lk 5:18-26

Jesus heals and forgives paralytic man

Matthew: Jesus stepped into a boat, crossed over and came to his own town. (Capernaum) Some men brought to him a paralytic, lying on a mat. When Jesus saw their faith, he said to the paralytic, "Take heart son your sins are forgiven." At this, some of the teachers of the law said to themselves, "This fellow is blaspheming!" Knowing their thoughts, Jesus said, "Why do you entertain evil thoughts in your hearts? Which is easier: to say Your sins are forgiven, or to say, Get up and walk, but that you should know that the Son of Man has authority on earth to forgive sins Then he said to the paralytic, "Get up, take up your bed and go home." And the man got up and went home.

| 153 | 6th day | Tammuz 24 | **Matthew's Home** |

Mt 9:9-13   Mk 2:13-17   Lk 5:27-32

Jesus calls Matthew to follow him
and eats dinner at his home

Matthew: As Jesus went on from there, he saw a man sitting at the tax collectors booth and said, "Follow me" and Matthew got up and followed him.

| 154 | Sabbath | Tammuz 25 | **Matthew's Home** |

Week Twenty-Three
Year 27 AD

| 155 | 1th day | Tammuz 26 | **Town to Town** |

Mt 10:1-15   Mk 6:7-13   Lk 9:1-6

Sends out the twelve Disciples

Matthew: Then he called his twelve disciples to him and gave them authority to drive out evil spirits and to heal every disease and sickness. ...Vs5 These twelve Jesus sent out with the following instructions: "Do not go among the gentiles or enter any town of the Samaritans. Go rather to the lost sheep of Israel."

156	2nd Day	Tammuz 27	**Town to Town**
157	3rd Day	Tammuz 28	**Tour of Galilee**
158	4th Day	Tammuz 29	**Tour of Galilee**
159	5th Day	Av 01	**Tour of Galilee**
160	6th Day	Av 02	**Tour of Galilee**
161	Sabbath	Av 03	**Tour of Galilee**

Week Twenty-Four
Year 27 AD

| 162 | 1th day | Av 04 | **Town to Town** |

Mt 10:1-15   Mk 6:7-13   Lk 9:1-6

Sends out the twelve Disciples

Matthew: Then he called his twelve disciples to him and gave them authority to drive out evil spirits and to heal every disease and sickness. ...Vs5 These twelve Jesus sent out with the following instructions: "Do not go among the gentiles or enter any town of the Samaritans. Go rather to the lost sheep of Israel."

163	2nd Day	Av 05	**Tour of Galilee**
164	3rd Day	Av 06	**Tour of Galilee**
165	4th Day	Av 07	**Tour of Galilee**
166	5th Day	Av 08	**Tour of Galilee**

167	6th Day	Av 09	**Tour of Galilee**
168	Sabbath	Av 10	**Tour of Galilee**

Week Twenty-Five
Year 27 AD

169	1st day	Av 11	**Town to Town**

Mt 10:1-15   Mk 6:7-13   Lk 9:1-6

Sends out the twelve Disciples

Matthew: Then he called his twelve disciples to him and gave them authority to drive out evil spirits and to heal every disease and sickness. …Vs5 These twelve Jesus sent out with the following instructions: "Do not go among the gentiles or enter any town of the Samaritans. Go rather to the lost sheep of Israel."

170	2nd Day	Av 12	**Tour of Galilee**
171	3rd Day	Av 13	**Tour of Galilee**
172	4th Day	Av 14	**Tour of Galilee**
173	5th Day	Av 15	**Tour of Galilee**
174	6th Day	Av 16	**Tour of Galilee**
175	Sabbath	Av 17	**Tour of Galilee**

Week Twenty-Six
Year 27 AD

| 176 | 1st day | Av 18 | **Town to Town** |

Mt 10:1-15   Mk 6:7-13   Lk 9:1-6

Sends out the twelve Disciples

Matthew: Then he called his twelve disciples to him and gave them authority to drive out evil spirits and to heal every disease and sickness. …Vs5 These twelve Jesus sent out with the following instructions: "Do not go among the gentiles or enter any town of the Samaritans. Go rather to the lost sheep of Israel."

| 177 | 2nd day | Av 19 | **Tour of Galilee** |

Mt 10:16-42

Matthew: Jesus speaking, "Be on your guard against men they will hand you over to the local councils and flog you in their synagogues, on my account."

| 178 | 3rd day | Av 20 | Galilee |

Mt 11:1   Lk 7:18-35

Matthew: after Jesus had finished instructing his twelve disciples, he went on from there to teach and preach in the towns of Galilee.

179	4th Day	Av 21	**Tour of Galilee**
180	5th Day	Av 22	**Tour of Galilee**
181	6th Day	Av 23	**Tour of Galilee**
182	Sabbath	Av 24	**Tour of Galilee**

Week Twenty-Seven
Year 27 AD

| 183 | 1st day | Av 25 | **Tour of Galilee** |

Mt 11:1   Lk 7:18-35

Matthew: After Jesus had finished instructing his twelve disciples, he went on from there to teach and preach in the towns of Galilee.

184	2nd Day	Av 26	**Town to Town**
185	3rd Day	Av 27	**Tour of Galilee**
186	4th Day	Av 28	**Tour of Galilee**
187	5th Day	Av 29	**Tour of Galilee**
188	6th Day	Av 30	**Tour of Galilee**
189	Sabbath	Elul 01	**Tour of Galilee**

Week Twenty-Eight
Year 27 AD

| 190 | 1st Day | Elul 02 | **Galilee** |

Mt 11:1   Lk 7:18-35

Matthew: After Jesus had finished instructing his twelve disciples, he went on from there to teach and preach in the towns of Galilee.

| 191 | 2nd Day | Elul 03 | **Town to Town** |
| 192 | 3rd Day | Elul 04 | **Tour of Galilee** |

193	4th Day	Elul 05	**Tour of Galilee**
194	5th Day	Elul 06	**Tour of Galilee**
195	6th Day	Elul 07	**Tour of Galilee**
196	Sabbath	Elul 08	**Tour of Galilee**

Week Twenty-Nine
Year 27 AD

197	1st day	Elul 09	**Galilee**

Mt 11:1   Lk 7:18-35

Matthew After Jesus had finished instructing his twelve disciples, he went on from there to teach and preach in the towns of Galilee.

197	2nd Day	Elul 10	**From Jerusalem**

Mt 14:1-12   Mk 6:14-29   Lk 9:7-9

Matthew: At that time Herod, the tetrarch heard the reports about Jesus and he said to his attendants, "This is John the Baptist, he has risen from the dead! That is why the miraculous powers are at work in him."

199	3rd Day	Elul 11	**Herod in Jerusalem**

Mt 14:13

Matthew: When Jesus heard what had happened, he withdrew by boat, privately, to a solitary place.

200	6th Day	Elul 12	**Herod in Jerusalem**

Mt 14:13

Matthew: When Jesus heard what had happened, he

withdrew by boat, privately, to a solitary place.

| 201 | 5th Day | Elul 13 | **Capernaum** |

Mk 6:30

Apostles return from mission trip in Galilee

Mark: The apostles gathered around Jesus and reported to him all they had done and taught (on their trips). Then because so many people were coming and going that they did not do nor even have a chance to eat, Jesus said, "Come with me by yourselves to a quiet place and get some rest."

| 202 | 6th Day | Elul 14 | **Capernaum** |
| 203 | Sabbath | Elul 15 | **Capernaum** |

Week Thirty
Year 27 AD

204	1st Day	Elul 16	**Capernaum**
205	2nd Day	Elul 17	**By Sea of Galilee**
206	3rd Day	Elul 18	**By Sea of Galilee**
207	4th Day	Elul 19	**By Sea of Galilee**
208	5th Day	Elul 20	**By Sea of Galilee**
209	6th Day	Elul 21	**By Sea of Galilee**
210	Sabbath	Elul 22	**Capernaum**

Week Thirty-One
Year 27 AD

211	1st Day	Elul 23	**Sea of Galilee Area**
212	2nd Day	Elul 24	**Mountain by Sea**

Mt 14:14   Mk 6:30-44   Lk 9:10-17   Jn 6:1-14

**Feeding of the five thousand,
not counting women and children.**

Matthew: When Jesus landed and saw a large crowd: he (Jesus) had compassion on them and healed their sick. As evening approached, the disciples came to him and said, "This is a remote place, and it's already getting late. Send the crowds away, so they can go to the villages and buy themselves some food." Jesus said, "They don't need to go away. You give them something to eat " vs. 17 "We have here only five loaves of bread (leavened) and two fish" Jesus said, "Bring them to me"

He directed the disciples to have them sit in groups of fifty and they all ate and were satisfied and the disciples gathered up 12 baskets extra.

213	3rd Day	Elul 25	**Sea of Galilee**

Jn 6:15

John: Jesus knowing that they intended to come and make him king by force withdrew again to a mountain by himself.

214	4th Day	Elul 26	**Near Bethsaida**

Mt 14:22-27   Mk 6:45-52

Jesus walking on the water

Mark: Immediately, Jesus made the disciples get into the boat and go on, ahead of him, to the other side, while he dismissed the crowd. …. But the boat was a considerable distance from land. Vs. 26 when the disciples saw him walking on the lake, they were terrified. …Vs. 27 But Jesus immediately said to them: "Take courage, It is I, Don't be afraid " "Lord if it is you" Peter replied " tell me to come to you on the water." Jesus said "Come".

| 215 | 5th Day | Elul 27 | **Genneserat** |

Mt 14:34-36
Jesus healed all their sick

Matthew: When they had crossed over they landed at Genneserat. And when the men of that place recognized Jesus, … people brought all their sick to him and begged him to let the sick just touch edge of his cloak, and all who touched him were healed.

| 216 | 6th day | Elul 28 | **Galilee** |

Mt 15:1-9   Mk 7:1-13
Why don't your disciples wash their hands?

Matthew: Then some Pharisees and teachers of the law came to Jesus from Jerusalem and asked, "Why do your disciples break the tradition of the elders? They don't wash their hands before they eat? Jesus replied, "And why do you break the command of GOD for the sake of your tradition? Thus you nullify the word of GOD for the sake of your tradition. GOD's law forbids adding to his laws for his people".

| 217 | Sabbath | Elul 29 | **Capernaum** |

Mt 15:10   Mk 7:14-20

**Still speaking to Pharisees, teachers, and people
in the synagogue**

Matthew: Jesus called the crowd to him and said, "Listen and understand, What goes into a man's mouth does not make him unclean, but what comes out of his mouth, that is what makes him unclean".

Week Thirty-Two
Year 27 AD
First of the Fall Feasts
Leviticus 23:23
Yom Teruah, Day of Trumpets

This feast does not occur on a pre-set date, because it is celebrated at the sighting of the renewed moon in the heavens

| 218 | 1st Day | Tishri 01 | **To Tyre** |

Mt 15:21-28   Mk 7:24-30

**Gentile woman begs Jesus
to deliver her daughter and he does.**

Mark: Leaving that place Jesus withdrew to the region of Tyre and Sidon

Mark: ...vs. 26 the woman was a Greek ...She begged Jesus to drive the demon out of her daughter. First let the children eat all they want, he told her, "for it is not right to take the children's bread and toss it to their dogs." Yes

Lord, she replied, but even the dogs under the table eat the children's crumbs.

Then Jesus told her, "For such a reply you may go: the demon has left your daughter".
　　　(Tyre is about 35 miles from Capernaum
　　　and is a Gentile region on the Mediterranean)

| 219 | 2nd Day | Tishri 02 | **To Sea of Galilee** |

Mt 15:29-31　　Mk 7:29-31
**Jesus makes spittle with dirt
and heals a man's blindness**

Mark: Then Jesus left the vicinity of Tyre and went through Sidon, down to the Sea of Galilee and into the region of the Decapolis (10 cities on the far side of the sea) there some people brought to him a man who was deaf and could hardly talk. Jesus took him away from the crowd, and then he spit and touched the man's tongue and with a deep sigh said to him "Ephrata"! Which means "be opened" At this, the man's ears were opened, his tongue was loosened and he began to speak plainly.

| 220 | 3rd Day | Tishri 03 | **Near Sea of Galilee** |
| 221 | 4th Day | Tishri 04 | **Near Sea of Galilee** |

Mt 15:32-39　　Mk 8:1-8
Feeding the four thousand

Mark: During those days another large crowd gathered. Since they had nothing to eat, Jesus called his disciples to him and said, "I have compassion for these people: they have already been with me three days and have nothing to eat. If I send them home hungry, they will collapse on the way, because some of them have come along distance

| 222 | 5th Day | Tishri 05 | **Mt. Tabor** |

Mt 17:1-13   Mk 9:2-13   Lk 9:28-36

Transfiguration

Matthew: After six days Jesus took with him Peter, James, and John...and led them up a high Mountain by themselves. There he was transfigured before them. His face shone like the sun, and his clothes become as white as the light. Just then there appeared before them Moses and Elijah talking with Jesus.

| 223 | 6th Day | Tishri 06 | **Galilee** |

Mt 17:14-21   Mk 9:14-29   Lk 9:37-45

Jesus delivers a son from an evil spirit for a father.

Luke: The next day, when they came down from the mountain, a large crowd met him...Teacher, I beg you to look at my son for he is my only child. A spirit seizes him and he suddenly screams. It throws him into convulsions.... But Jesus rebuked the evil spirit, healed the boy and gave him back to his father. And they were amazed at the greatness of GOD.

| 224 | Sabbath | Tishri 07 | **Galilee** |

Week Thirty-Three
Year 27 AD

| 225 | 1st Day | Tishri 08 | **Galilee** |

Mt 17:14-22   Mk 9:20-32   Lk 9:44-45

Jesus predicts his death and resurrection.

Luke: They left that place and passed through Galilee, Jesus did not want any one to know where they were, because he was teaching his disciples.

Luke 9:43 Jesus said to them, "The Son of Man is going to be betrayed into the hands of men. They will kill him, and after three days and he will rise." But they did not understand what he meant.

| 226 | 2nd Day | Tishri 09 | **Capernaum** |

Mt 17:24-27

Jesus tells Peter how to pay their taxes by fishing

Matthew: After Jesus and his disciples arrived in Capernaum, the collectors of the two-drachma tax came to Peter and asked "Doesn't your teacher pay the Temple tax." When Peter came into the house, Jesus was the first to speak. "What do you think, Simon? From whom do the kings of this earth collect duty and taxes from their own sons or from others" From others", Peter answered. …Vs27 Jesus said, "But that we may not offend them, go to the lake and throw out your line. Take the first fish you catch: open its mouth and you will find a four-drachma coin. Take it and give it to them for my tax and yours".

| 227 | 3rd Day | Tishri 10 | **Capernaum** |

The Holiest Day of the year, "Yom Kippur", the Day of Atonement is a total fast ending the 40 days of

Repentance, and also ending the ten days of awe. (Leviticus 23:26-32)
This day is of such importance, because if everything is not done as GOD has commanded, the sins of all Israel may not be covered.

To safeguard the High Priest from being defiled, he is kept in seclusion at the Temple for a week before the Holy Day, and a second Priest is also secluded in case of the death or

The Seventy-Week Ministry, 112

Short trips from Capernaum and Third trip to Jerusalem For the Feast of Tabernacles (Sukkots)

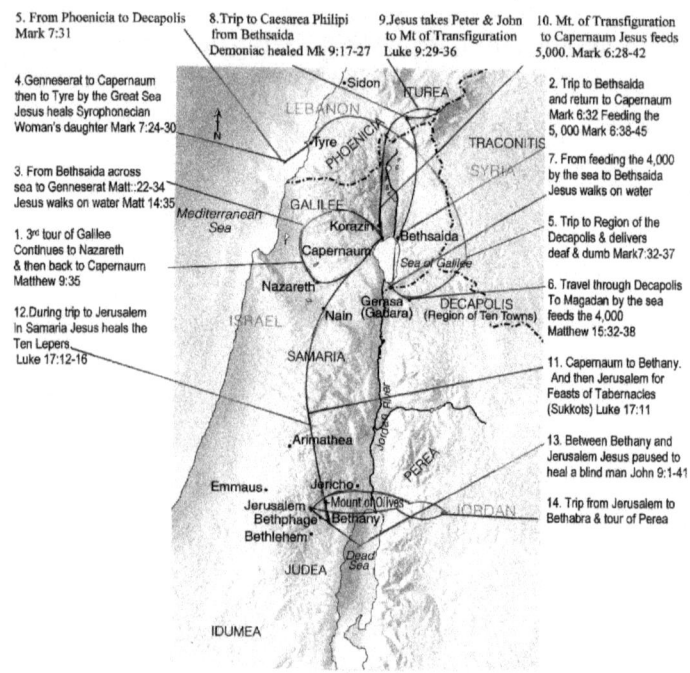

5. From Phoenicia to Decapolis Mark 7:31

8. Trip to Caesarea Philipi from Bethsaida Demoniac healed Mk 9:17-27

9. Jesus takes Peter & John to Mt of Transfiguration Luke 9:29-36

10. Mt. of Transfiguration to Capernaum Jesus feeds 5,000. Mark 6:28-42

4. Genneserat to Capernaum then to Tyre by the Great Sea Jesus heals Syrophonecian Woman's daughter Mark 7:24-30

3. From Bethsaida across sea to Genneserat Matt::22-34 Jesus walks on water Matt 14:35

1. 3rd tour of Galilee Continues to Nazareth & then back to Capernaum Matthew 9:35

12. During trip to Jerusalem In Samaria Jesus heals the Ten Lepers. Luke 17:12-18

2. Trip to Bethsaida and return to Capernaum Mark 6:32 Feeding the 5, 000 Mark 6:38-45

7. From feeding the 4,000 by the sea to Bethsaida Jesus walks on water

5. Trip to Region of the Decapolis & delivers deaf & dumb Mark7:32-37

6. Travel through Decapolis To Magadan by the sea feeds the 4,000 Matthew 15:32-38

11. Capernaum to Bethany. And then Jerusalem for Feasts of Tabernacles (Sukkots) Luke 17:11

13. Between Bethany and Jerusalem Jesus paused to heal a blind man John 9:1-41

14. Trip from Jerusalem to Bethabra & tour of Perea

defilement of the High Priest.

| 228 | 4th Day | Tishri 11 | **To Jerusalem** |

Jn 7:2

John: But when the Jewish Feast of Tabernacles (Translator's error: These are the Feasts of GOD) was near Jesus brothers said to him, "you ought to leave here and go to Judea, so that your disciples may see the miracles you do.... vs 10 However, after his brothers had left for the Feast, he went also, not publicly, but in secret.

| 229 | 5th Day | Tishri 12 | **To Jerusalem** |

Lk 9:51

Luke: As the time approached for him to be taken up to heaven, Jesus resolutely set out for Jerusalem

| 230 | 6th Day | Tishri 13 | **To Jerusalem** |

Before Sundown (beginning of High Sabbath) the pilgrims who have come to the Feast are busy building a leafy covering (Sukkah for the Feast of Sukkots) where they will sleep for the next eight nights.

| 231 | Sabbath | Tishri 14 | **Jerusalem** |

Week Thirty-Four
Year 27 AD
Feast of Tabernacles (Sukkots)

Continues with morning sacrifices and the water oblation to accompany prayers for rain.

| 232 | 1st Day | Tishri 15 | **Jerusalem** |

Feast Schedule:

First day of the Feast of Tabernacles (Sukkots). It is the most festive and joyful of all the Feasts. It is the Feast most mentioned in scripture and the shadow pictures of the Feast are the backdrop for the Lord's return and teaching in John 7-9 This Feast of Yahweh is to commemorate the provision of GOD for everything needed for the forty years in the wilderness, when they lived in small huts.

Yahweh's Feast of Tabernacles is an 8-day feast Centered on GOD's provision for the harvest of the grains, fruits, and nuts and for GOD's provision during the forty years in the wilderness. The first and eighth days are a High Sabbath, (a day without work) and on the latter there is the prayer for rain for the crops of the next year.
This feast was a required attendance in Jerusalem.

| 233 | 2nd Day | Tishri 16 | **Jerusalem** |

Jn 8:12

Feast Schedule 2nd day

John: When Jesus spoke again to the people he said, "I am the light of the world, whoever follows me will never walk in darkness, but will have the light of life."

Feast Schedule: Starting with the second day of the Feast, a festive and elaborate lighting ceremony with the Levites singing fifteen Psalms (#120-#134) as they descend 15 steps with the fire to light the Menorah's in the Temple. This celebration was reminder of the descending of the Shekinah Glory of the Lord in Ezekiel 43:1-6

| 234 | 3rd Day | Tishri 17 | **Jerusalem** |

Jn 7:14-19
Feast Schedule 3rd day
John: Not until halfway through the Feast did Jesus go up to the temple courts and begin to teach. Vs 15 The Jews were amazed and asked, "How did this man (Jesus) get such learning without having studied".... vs 19 Jesus speaking, "Has not Moses given you the law? Yet not one of you keeps the law. Why are you trying to kill me"?

| 235 | 4th Day | Tishri 18 | **Jerusalem** |

Jn 7:23-24
Feast Schedule 4th day
John: Now if a child can be circumcised on the Sabbath so that the Law of Moses may not be broken, why are you angry with me for healing the whole man on the Sabbath?

| 236 | 5th Day | Tishri 19 | **Jerusalem** |

Jn 7:25-29
Feast Schedule 5th day
Jesus speaking publicly after the Pharisees said he should be arrested and killed

John: ... Isn't this the man, they are trying to kill? Here he is speaking publicly, and they are not saying a word to him. Have the Authorities really concluded that he is the Christ. Vs 27 But we know where this man is from? When the Christ comes, no one will know where he is from. Then Jesus still teaching in the temple courts, cried out. "Yes, you know me and you know where I am from, I am not here on my own, but he who sent me is true. You do not know him, but I know him, because I am from him and he sent me."

Vs 30 at this they tried to seize him, but no one laid a hand on him, because his time had not come. Still many in the crowd put their faith in him. They said, " When the Christ comes, will he do more miraculous signs than this man."

237	6th Day	Tishri 20	Jerusalem
Feast Schedule 6th day			
238	Sabbath	Tishri 21	Jerusalem

Week Thirty-Five
Year 27 AD

239	1st Day	Tishri 22	Jerusalem

Jn 7:37-40

Feast Schedule: The "Last Great Day"

The special prayer service for rain where the High pries takes the golden laver down to the pool of Shiloam to get some water and bring it back to the altar and pour it from corner to corner. The streets are lined with pilgrims and priests worshiping GOD asking GOD to bring the rains. Then John's Gospel tells us about the Lord's loud offer to the Jews.

John: On the last and greatest day of the Feast, Jesus stood and said in a loud voice, " If anyone is thirsty, let him come to me and drink. Whoever believes in me as the Scripture has said, streams of living water will flow from within him."…Vs. 40 on hearing his words, some of the people said, "Surely this man is The Prophet."

| 240 | 2nd Day | Tishri 23 | **Jerusalem** |

Lk 10:1-16
Jesus sends out 70 or 72 in pairs to prepare the way
Luke: After this the Lord appointed seventy two others(some versions say 70) and sent them two by two ahead of him into every town and place where he was about to go.

241	3rd Day	Tishri 24	**Judea and Perea**
242	4th Day	Tishri 25	**Judea and Perea**
243	5th Day	Tishri 26	**Judea and Perea**
244	6th Day	Tishri 27	**Judea and Perea**
245	Sabbath	Tishri 28	**Judea and Perea**

Week Thirty-Six
Year 27 AD

Judea and Perea seem to be the areas of the ministry tour for the 72 disciples sent out to prepare the way for Jesus. Jesus is out preaching and healing all that were sick in the towns and villages he had sent out the 72 disciples.

246	1st Day	Tishri 29	**Judea and Perea**
247	2nd Day	Tishri 30	**Judea and Perea**
248	3rd Day	Heshwan 01	**Judea and Perea**

249	4th Day	Heshwan 02	**Judea and Perea**
250	5th Day	Heshwan 03	**Judea and Perea**
251	6th Day	Heshwan 04	**Judea and Perea**
252	Sabbath	Heshwan 05	**Judea and Perea**

Week Thirty-Seven
Year 27 AD

Judea and Perea seem to be the areas of the ministry tour for the 72 disciples sent out to prepare the way for Jesus. Jesus is out preaching and healing all that were sick in the towns and villages he had sent out the 72 disciples.

252	1st Day	Heshwan 06	**Judea and Perea**
253	2nd Day	Heshwan 07	**Judea and Perea**
254	3rd Day	Heshwan 08	**Judea and Perea**
255	4th Day	Heshwan 09	**Judea and Perea**
256	5th Day	Heshwan 10	**Judea and Perea**
257	6th Day	Heshwan 11	**Judea and Perea**
258	Sabbath	Heshwan 12	**Judea and Perea**

Week Thirty-Eight
Year 27 AD

Judea and Perea seem to be the areas of the ministry tour for the 72 disciples sent out to prepare the way for Jesus.

Jesus is out preaching and healing all that were sick in the towns and villages he had sent out the 72 disciples.

260	1st Day	Heshwan 13	**Judea and Perea**
261	2nd Day	Heshwan 14	**Judea and Perea**
262	3rd Day	Heshwan 15	**Judea and Perea**
263	4th Day	Heshwan 16	**Judea and Perea**
264	5th day	Heshwan 17	**Judea and Perea**
265	6th Day	Heshwan 18	**Judea and Perea**
266	Sabbath	Heshwan 19	**Judea and Perea**

Week Thirty-Nine
Year 27 AD

Judea and Perea seem to be the areas of the ministry tour for the 72 disciples sent out to prepare the way for Jesus. Jesus is out preaching and healing all that were sick in the towns and villages he had sent out the 72 disciples.

267	1st Day	Heshwan 20	**Judea and Perea**
268	2nd Day	Heshwan 21	**Judea and Perea**
269	3rd Day	Heshwan 22	**Judea and Perea**
270	4th Day	Heshwan 23	**Judea and Perea**
271	5th Day	Heshwan 24	**Judea and Perea**

| 272 | 6th Day | Heshwan 25 | **Judea and Perea** |
| 273 | Sabbath | Heshwan 26 | **Judea and Perea** |

Week Forty
Year 27 AD

Judea and Perea seem to be the areas of the ministry tour for the 72 disciples sent out to prepare the way for Jesus. Jesus is out preaching and healing all that were sick in the towns and villages he had sent out the 72 disciples.

274	1st Day	Heshwan 27	**Judea and Perea**
275	2nd Day	Heshwan 28	**Judea and Perea**
276	3rd Day	Heshwan 29	**Judea and Perea**
277	4th Day	Kislev 01	**Judea and Perea**
278	5th Day	Kislev 02	**Judea and Perea**
279	6th Day	Kislev 03	**Judea and Perea**
280	Sabbath	Kislev 04	**Judea and Perea**

Week Forty-One
Year 27 AD

Judea and Perea seem to be the areas of the ministry tour for the 72 disciples sent out to prepare the way for Jesus. Jesus is out preaching and healing all that were sick in the towns and villages he had sent out the 72 disciples.

281	1st Day	Kislev 05	**Perea Trans-Jordan**
282	2nd Day	Kislev 06	**Perea Trans-Jordan**
283	3rd Day	Kislev 07	**Perea Trans-Jordan**
284	4th Day	Kislev 08	**Perea Trans-Jordan**
285	5th Day	Kislev 09	**Perea Trans-Jordan**
286	6th Day	Kislev 10	**Perea Trans-Jordan**

Lk 13:10-13
Jesus heals the crippled woman on the Sabbath
Luke: On a Sabbath Jesus was teaching in one of the Synagogues, and a woman was there who had been crippled by a spirit for eighteen years...vs. 12 When Jesus saw her, he called her forward and said to her, "Woman you are set free from your infirmity."

| 287 | Sabbath | Kislev 11 | **Trans-Jordan** |

Lk 13:14-16
Ruler of the Synagogue rebukes Jesus
for healing on the Sabbath
Luke: Indignant because Jesus had healed on the Sabbath, the synagogue ruler said to the people, "There are six days for work. So come and be healed on those days not on the Sabbath." The Lord answered him, "You hypocrites! Doesn't each of you on the Sabbath untie his ox or donkey from the stall and lead it out to give it water. Then should not this woman, a daughter of Abraham, whom satan has kept bound for eighteen long years, be set free on the

The Seventy-Week Ministry, 122

Fourth and Fifth trip to Jerusalem
For the Feast of Passover

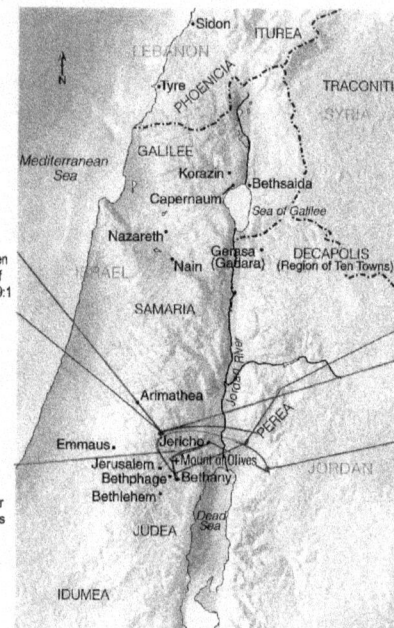

4. Galilee to Perea
Jesus heals the woman
Of her infirmity. Luke 13:11

3. Ephraim into Galilee & then
to Judea on the other side of
the Jordan River Matthew 19:1

6. Jericho to Bethany &
Jerusalem for Final Passover
Jesus heals Blind Bartimeaus
Mark 10:46-52

1. Bethabra to Bethany.
Jesus heals Lazarus
John 11:1-46

2. Bethany to Ephraim
Jesus Left because the
Pharisees want to kill him.
And the Barley is not ripe.

5. Trip to Jericho
Jesus blesses the Children
from Perea Luke.18:15-17

Sabbath day from what bound her."

Week Forty-Two
Year 27 AD

Judea and Perea seem to be the areas of the ministry tour for the 72 disciples sent out to prepare the way for Jesus. Jesus is out preaching and healing all that were sick in the towns and villages he had sent out the 72 disciples.

| 288 | 1st Day | Kislev 12 | **Trans-Jordan** |

Lk 13:17

Luke: When he said this, all his opponents were humiliated, but the people were delighted with all the wonderful things he (Jesus) was doing.

290	2nd Day	Kislev 13	**Bethabra**
291	3rd Day	Kislev 14	**To Jerusalem**
292	4th Day	Kislev 15	**To Jerusalem**
293	5th Day	Kislev 16	**To Jerusalem**
294	6th Day	Kislev 17	**Jerusalem**
295	Sabbath	Kislev 18	**Jerusalem**

Jn 9:1-12
Jesus heals the man born blind.

John: As (Jesus) he went along, he saw a man blind from birth. The disciples asked him, Rabbi, who sinned, this man or his parents, that he was born blind. Jesus speaking, "Neither, this man nor his parents sinned, but this happened so that the work of GOD might be displayed in his life.

Vs 6 Having said this Jesus spit on the ground, and made some mud with his saliva, and put it on the mans eyes. "Go! Wash in the Pool of Siloam". So the man went and washed and came home seeing.

Week Forty-Three
Year 27 AD
Hanukkah
The Feast of Dedication
The Feast of Lights

Hanukkah, The Festival of Lights, is not a Feast that the GOD has appointed to meet his children in Jerusalem but a Feast to celebrate the Dedication of the Temple back to the service of GOD.

295	1st Day	Kislev 19	**Jerusalem**

Jn 9:13-34

John: they brought to the Pharisees the man who had been blind. Now the day on which Jesus had made the mud and opened the mans eyes was a Sabbath…. vs. 30 the man answered, "Now that is remarkable! You don't know where he comes from, but he opened my eyes. We know that GOD does not listen to sinners. He listens to the godly man who does his will. Nobody has ever heard of opening the eyes of a man born blind. If this man were not from GOD, he could do nothing.

| 296 | 2nd Day | Kislev 20 | **Jerusalem** |

Jn 9:35-41

John: Jesus heard that the Pharisees had thrown the healed man out of the Synagogue and when he found him he said, " Do you believe in the Son of Man?" Who is he, Sir? The man said, " Tell me, so that I may believe in him." Jesus said, "You have now seen him, in fact, he is the one speaking with you."

| 297 | 3rd day | Kislev 21 | **Jerusalem** |

Jn 10:22-30
Feast schedule Day 1

John: Then came the Feast of Dedication (Feast of Lights or Hanukkah) at Jerusalem. It was winter, and Jesus was in the temple area walking in Solomon's Colonnade. Vs 24 The Jews gathered around him, saying, " How long will you keep us in suspense? If you are the Christ, tell us plainly". Jesus answered, " I did tell you, but you did not believe. The miracles I do in my Father's name speak for me but you do not believe because you are not my sheep."

| 298 | 4th Day | Kislev 22 | **Jerusalem** |

Jn 10:31-33
Feast Schedule Day 2

John: Again the Jews picked up stones to stone him, but Jesus said to them, "I have shown you many great miracles from the Father. For which of these (miracles) do you stone me?'

| 299 | 5th Day | Kislev 23 | **Jerusalem** |

Feast Schedule Day 3

| 300 | 6th Day | Kislev 24 | **Jerusalem** |

Feast Schedule Day 4

| 301 | Sabbath | Kislev 25 | **Jerusalem** |

Feast Schedule Day 5

Week Forty-Four
Year 27 AD
Feast of Hanukkah (Dedication)

| 302 | 1st Day | Kislev 26 | **Jerusalem** |

Feast schedule: Day 6

| 303 | 2nd Day | Kislev 27 | **Jerusalem** |

Jn 10:40

Feast schedule: Day 7

John: Then Jesus went back across the Jordan to the place where John the Baptist had been baptizing in the early days.

| 304 | 3rd Day | Kislev 28 | **Trans-Jordan** |

Feast schedule Day 8

305	4th Day	Kislev 29	**Trans-Jordan**
306	5th Day	Kislev 30	**Trans-Jordan**
307	6th Day	Teveth 01	**Trans-Jordan**

| 308 | Sabbath | Teveth 02 | **Trans-Jordan** |

Week Forty-Five
Year 27 AD

309	1st Day	Teveth 03	**Trans-Jordan**
310	2nd Day	Teveth 04	**Trans-Jordan**
311	3rd Day	Teveth 05	**Trans-Jordan**
312	4th day	Teveth 06	**Trans-Jordan**

Lk 13:22-30

Luke: Then Jesus went through the towns and villages (long trip) teaching as he made his way to Jerusalem.

| 313 | 5th Day | Teveth 07 | **Trans-Jordan** |
| 314 | 6th Day | Teveth 08 | **Trans-Jordan** |

Lk13:31

Jesus sorrow for Jerusalem

Luke: At this time some Pharisees came to Jesus and said to him, "Leave this place and go somewhere else. Herod wants to kill you.".... Vs. 34 O Jerusalem, Jerusalem, you who kill the prophets and stone those sent to you, how often I have longed to gather your children together as a hen gathers her chicks under her wings, but you were not willing! Look your house is left to you desolate I tell you, you will not see me again until you say "Blessed is he who comes in the name of the Lord."

| 315 | Sabbath | Teveth 09 | **Trans-Jordan** |

Week Forty-Six
Year 27 AD

316	1st Day	Teveth 10	**Trans-Jordan**
317	2nd Day	Teveth 11	**Bethabra Area**
318	3rd Day	Teveth 12	**Bethabra Area**
319	4th Day	Teveth 13	**Bethabra Area**
320	5th Day	Teveth 14	**Bethabra Area**
321	6th Day	Teveth 15	**Bethabra Area**
322	Sabbath	Teveth 16	**Trans-Jordan**

Lk 14:1-6

Jesus heals the man with dropsy on the Sabbath at a Pharisee's house

Luke: One Sabbath, when Jesus went to eat in the house of a prominent Pharisees, he was being carefully watched. There in front of him was a man suffering from dropsy. Jesus asked the Pharisee, " is it lawful to heal on the Sabbath or not?" But they remained silent, so taking hold of the men: he healed him and sent him away. Then he asked them, "If one of you has a son or an ox that falls into a well on the Sabbath day, will you not immediately pull him out."

Week Forty-Seven
Year 27 AD

323	1st Day	Teveth 17	**Trans-Jordan**
324	2nd Day	Teveth 18	**Trans-Jordan**

Lk 14:25-34

Jesus teaches about the cost of being a disciple

Luke: In the same way, any of you who does not give up everything he has, cannot be my disciple.

325	3rd Day	Teveth 19	**Trans-Jordan**
326	4th Day	Teveth 20	**Trans-Jordan**
327	5th Day	Teveth 21	**Trans-Jordan**
328	6th Day	Teveth 22	**Trans-Jordan**
329	Sabbath	Teveth 23	**Trans-Jordan**

Week Forty-Eight
Year 27 AD

330	1st Day	Teveth 24	**To Jerusalem**

Luke: Jesus teaching in towns and villages
    Parables: The Great Supper
        14:15-24
  Counting the cost
    14:25-33
        The Lost Sheep
           15:1-7
        The Prodigal Son

15:8-10
The Lost Coin
15:11-32
Unjust Steward
16:1-13
Dives and Lazarus
16:19-31

331	2nd Day	Teveth 25	**To Jerusalem**
332	3rd Day	Teveth 26	**To Jerusalem**
333	4th Day	Teveth 27	**To Jerusalem**
334	5th Day	Teveth 28	**To Jerusalem**
335	6th Day	Teveth 29	**To Jerusalem**
336	Sabbath	Shevat 01	**To Jerusalem**

Week Forty-Nine
Year 27 AD

| 337 | 1st Day | Shevat 02 | **Beyond the Jordan** |

Jn 11:1-9

Jesus hears that Lazarus is sick

John: Now a man named Lazarus was sick. He was from Bethany the village of Mary and her sister Martha…. vs3 So the sisters sent word to Jesus, Lord the one you love is sick. When he heard this Jesus said, " This sickness will not end in death. No it is for GOD's glory So that the GOD's Son may be glorified through it.

338	2nd Day	Shevat 03	**To Bethany**
339	3rd Day	Shevat 04	**Bethany**
340	4th Day	Shevat 05	**Bethany**
341	5th Day	Shevat 06	**Bethany**

Jn 11:38-45

Jesus raises Lazarus from the dead

John: Father I thank you that you always hear me, but I said this for the benefit of the people standing here, that they may believe that you sent me. When he had said this, Jesus called, "Lazarus come forth"! The dead man came out and his hands and his feet wrapped with strips of linen and a cloth around his face. Jesus said to them, "Take off the grave clothes and let him go".

342	6th Day	Shevat 07	**Bethany**
343	Sabbath	Shevat 08	**Bethany**

Week Fifty
Year 27 AD

344	1st Day	Shevat 09	**Bethany**

Jn 11:45-50

The plot to kill Jesus

John: Therefore many of the Jews who had come to visit Mary and had seen what Jesus did, put their faith in him. But some of them went to the Pharisees and told them what Jesus had done. …. Then the chief priests and the

Pharisees called a meeting of the Sanhedrin.... Here this man is performing miraculous signs vs 48 If we let him go on like this, everyone will believe. Vs.50 You do not realize that it is better for you, that one man die for the people than the whole nation perish.

345	2nd Day	Shevat 10	**Bethany**
346	3rd Day	Shevat 11	**Bethany**
347	4th Day	Shevat 12	**Bethany**
348	5th Day	Shevat 13	**Bethany**
349	6th Day	Shevat 14	**Bethany**
350	Sabbath	Shevat 15	**Bethany**

Week Fifty-One
Year 27 AD

351	1st Day	Shevat 16	**To Ephraim**

John 11:54: Therefore Jesus no longer moved about publicly among the Jews. Instead he withdrew to a region near the desert to a village called Ephraim where he stayed with his disciples.

352	2nd Day	Shevat 17	**To Ephraim**
353	3rd Day	Shevat 18	**Ephraim**
354	4th Day	Shevat 19	**Ephraim**
355	5th Day	Shevat 20	**Ephraim**

356	6th Day	Shevat 21	**Ephraim**
357	Sabbath	Shevat 22	**Ephraim**

Week Fifty-Two
Year 27 AD

358	1st Day	Shevat 23	**To Galilee**
359	2nd Day	Shevat 24	**Galilee**
360	3rd Day	Shevat 25	**Galilee**
361	4th Day	Shevat 26	**Galilee**
362	5th Day	Shevat 27	**Galilee**
363	6th Day	Shevat 28	**Galilee**
364	Sabbath	Shevat 29	**Galilee**

Week Fifty-Three
Year 27 AD

Note: There are no direct references to identify a town that Jesus visited after leaving Ephraim although the scriptures describing the woes to Korazin and Bethsaida in Matthew 11:20 and in Luke 10:23 indicate a possible visit at this time because Jesus speaks of the woes to these towns timed to be after his trip to Tyre and Sidon which was before the trip to Jerusalem for the Feast of Sukkots (Tabernacles).

365	1st Day	Shevat 30	**Galilee**
366	2nd Day	Adar 01	**Galilee**
367	3rd Day	Adar 02	**Galilee**
368	4th Day	Adar 03	**Galilee**
369	5th Day	Adar 04	**Galilee**
370	6th Day	Adar 05	**Galilee**
371	Sabbath	Adar 06	**Galilee**

Week Fifty-Four
Year 27 AD

372	1st Day	Adar 07	**Galilee**
373	2nd Day	Adar 08	**Galilee**
374	3rd Day	Adar 09	**Galilee**
375	4th Day	Adar 10	**Galilee**
376	5th Day	Adar 11	**Galilee**
377	6th Day	Adar 12	**Galilee**
378	Sabbath	Adar 13	**Galilee**

Week Fifty-Five
Year 27 AD

| 379 | 1st Day | Adar 14 | **Leaving Galilee** |

Luke 17:11-16: Jesus left Galilee for the last time
Now on the way to Jerusalem Jesus traveled along the border between Samaria and Galilee, as he was going into a village ten men who had leprosy, met him. They stood at a distance and called out in a loud voice, "Jesus, Master, have pity on us." Vs 14 when he saw them, he said, "Go show yourselves to the priests." And as they went they were cleansed.

380	2nd Day	Adar 15	**Galilee border**
381	3rd Day	Adar 16	**Galilee border**
382	4th Day	Adar 17	**Galilee border**
383	5th Day	Adar 18	**Galilee border**

Luke: Jesus teaching in towns and villages
Discourses on Forbearance Faith and Humility
Luke 17:20-27
Second Coming
Lk 17:20-27
Parable on Unjust Judge
Lk 18:1-14
Pharisee and the Publican
Lk 18:1-14

| 384 | 6th Day | Adar 19 | **Crossing Jordan** |

Mt. 19:1-12   Mk 10:1-12

Matthew 19:1-2: When Jesus had finished saying these things he left Galilee and went into the region of Judea to the other side of the Jordan. Vs 2 Large crowds followed him and he healed them there. Some Pharisees came to test him. They asked him, "is it lawful to divorce your wife for any and all reasons?" Jesus said no.

| 385 | Sabbath | Adar 20 | **Perea** |

Week Fifty-Six
Year 27 AD

| 386 | 1st Day | Adar 21 | **Perea** |

Mt. 19:13-15   Mk. 10:13-16   Lk. 18:15-17

Matthew 19:14-15: Then little children were brought to Jesus for him to place his hands on them and pray for them…. vs15 When he had placed his hands on them he went on from there.

| 387 | 2nd Day | Adar 22 | **Perea** |

Mt. 19:16-30   Mk. 10:17-31   Lk. 18:18-30

Mark: As Jesus started on his way, a man ran up to him and fell on his knees, before him Good teacher, he asked, "What must I do to inherit eternal life?"

388	3rd Day	Adar 23	**Perea**
389	4th Day	Adar 24	**Perea**
390	5th Day	Adar 25	**Perea**
391	6th Day	Adar 26	**Perea**
392	7th Day	Adar 27	**Perea**

Week Fifty-Seven
Year 27 AD

393	1st Day	Adar 28	**Perea**
394	2nd Day	Adar 29	**Perea**

Note: This year the Barley was not ripe and so a thirteenth month was added to the year 27 AD Certainly Jesus noticed and left also because it was not his time.

395	3rd Day	Adar II 01	**Perea**
396	4th Day	Adar II 02	**Perea**
397	5th Day	Adar II 03	**Perea**
398	6th Day	Adar II 04	**Perea**
399	Sabbath	Adar II 05	**Perea**

Week Fifty-Eight
Year 27 AD

400	1st Day	Adar II 06	**Perea**
401	2nd Day	Adar II 07	**Perea**
402	3rd Day	Adar II 08	**Perea**
403	4th Day	Adar II 09	**Perea**
404	5th Day	Adar II 10	**Perea**
405	6th Day	Adar II 11	**Perea**

| 406 | Sabbath | Adar II 12 | **Perea** |

Week Fifty-Nine
Year 27 AD

407	1st Day	Adar II 13	**Perea**
408	2nd Day	Adar II 14	**Perea**
409	3rd Day	Adar II 15	**Perea**

Purim:
A two-day feast celebrating
GOD's victory given to Esther and Mordecai

410	4th Day	Adar II 16	**Perea**
411	5th Day	Adar II 17	**Perea**
412	6th Day	Adar II 18	**Perea**
413	Sabbath	Adar II 19	**Perea**

Week Sixty
Year 27 AD

414	1st Day	Adar II 20	**Perea**
415	2nd Day	Adar II 21	**Perea**
416	3rd Day	Adar II 22	**Perea**
417	4th Day	Adar II 23	**Perea**

418	5th Day	Adar II 24	**Perea**
419	6th Day	Adar II 25	**Perea**
420	Sabbath	Adar II 26	**Perea**

Week Sixty-One
Year 27 AD

| 421 | 1st Day | Adar II 27 | **Near Jericho** |

Mt. 20:29-34   Mk. 10:46-52   Lk. 18:35-42

Jesus heals blind man on road to Jericho

Luke 18:39-40: As Jesus approached Jericho a blind man was sitting by the roadside begging. When he heard the crowd going by, he asked what was happening. They told him Jesus of Nazareth is passing by. He called out, "Jesus Son of David have mercy on me!" …Vs. 40 Jesus stopped and ordered the man to be brought to him…Jesus asked him, "What do you want me to do for you?" Lord, I want to see! Jesus said to him, " Receive your sight your faith has made you whole."

422	2nd Day	Adar II 28	**Near Jericho**
423	3rd Day	Adar II 29	**Near Jericho**
424	4th Day	Adar II 30	**Near Jericho**

Year 28 AD

The Head of the year, Rosh Hashanah

| 425 | 5th Day | Nisan 01 | **Entering Jericho** |

Lk.19:1-10

Jesus brings salvation to the house of Zacchaeus
Luke 19:1, 9: Jesus entered Jericho and was passing through: A man was there by the name of Zacchaeus. He was a chief tax collector and was wealthy. He was a short man ... he ran ahead and climbed a sycamore tree to see him (Jesus) When Jesus reached the tree he looked up and said to him, "Zacchaeus come down immediately, I must stay at your house today.... vs. 9 Jesus said to him, " Today Salvation has come to this house because this man too! Is a son of Abraham For the Son of Man came to seek and save that which was lost."

| 426 | 6th Day | Nisan 02 | **Jericho** |
| 427 | Sabbath | Nisan 03 | **Jericho** |

Week Sixty-Two
Year 28 AD

428	1st Day	Nisan 04	**Jericho**
429	2nd Day	Nisan 05	**Jericho**
430	3rd Day	Nisan 06	**Jericho**
431	4th Day	Nisan 07	**Jericho**
432	5th Day	Nisan 08	**Bethany**

Jn. 12:1-8

John 12:1, 3, 7: Six days before the Passover. Jesus

arrived in Bethany where Lazarus lived, whom Jesus had raised from the dead. Here a dinner was given in Jesus honor.... vs3 Then Mary took about a pint of pure nard, an expensive perfume, she poured it on Jesus feet and wiped it with her hair.... vs. 7 Jesus replied "Leave her alone it was intended that she should save this perfume for the day of my burial"

| 433 | 6th day | Nisan 09 | **Bethany** |

Mt. 21:1-5   Mk. 11:1-5   Lk. 19:28   Jn. 12:9-10

John 12:9-11: Meanwhile a large crowd of Jews found out that Jesus was there and came not only to see Lazarus, whom he had raised from the dead. Vs. 10 so the chief priests made plans to kill Lazarus as well, vs. 11 for on account of him of the Jews were going over to Jesus and putting their faith in him.

| 434 | Sabbath | Nisan 10 | **Jerusalem** |

Mt. 21:6-8   Mk. 11:5-10   Lk. 19:34-37   Jn. 12:12-15

Feast Preparation day number 1
Passover & Unleavened Bread
The choosing of the Passover Lamb

Exodus 12:2 Tell the whole community of Israel that on the tenth day of the month, each man is to take a lamb for his family, one for each household...vs. 6 take care of the (lambs) them until the fourteenth day of the month when all the people of the community of Israel must slaughter them at twilight.... vs. 8 that night they are to eat the meat roasted over the fire with bitter herbs and bread made without yeast.

The Triumphal Entry

John: The next day the great crowd that had come for the Feast (Passover, Unleavened Bread and First Fruits) heard that Jesus was on his way to Jerusalem. They took palm branches and went out to meet him, shouting "Hosanna" "Blessed is he who comes in the name of Lord, Blessed is the King of Israel"

Vs 14 Jesus found a young donkey and sat upon it, as it is written (in Zechariah 9:9)

Matthew: The disciples went and did as Jesus had instructed them. They brought the donkey and the colt, placed their cloaks on them, and Jesus sat on them.

Week Sixty-Three
Year 28 AD

Preparation starts on the 10th for the Feasts, which start on 14th day of the month and continues through the 22nd day of Nisan, the first month of the year, Passover, Unleavened Bread, and First Fruits. The Feasts end with a High Sabbath on the 22nd day.

435	1st Day	Nisan 11	**Jerusalem**

Cleansing the Temple of all leaven
Feast Preparation day number 2
Anointing of Jesus with perfumed oil

436	2nd Day	Nisan 12	**Jerusalem**

Feast Preparation day number 3

Questioning of Jesus by the Pharisees

| 437 | 3rd Day | Nisan 13 | **Jerusalem** |

Feast Preparation day number 4
The Last Supper happens at the end of this day.

After the sun goes down it is the beginning of Passover, the late night starts with prayer in the Garden of Gethsemane continuing into the daytime with the arrest, trial, crucifixion, and burial.

| 438 | 4th Day | Nisan 14 | **Jerusalem** |

Passover

The day of the Feast of Passover. Started at sundown the night of the thirteenth and ends with the death and burial of Jesus Christ at the twilight of the 14th day of Nisan along with the sacrifice of the Passover lambs for each family.

Each family sacrifices their lamb at twilight and eats the lamb with bitter herbs and unleavened bread. This meal starts at the end of the Passover day and ends well into the High Sabbath of Unleavened bread and Jehovah is praised for his deliverance of the Jewish people.

| 439 | 5th day | Nisan 15 | **Jerusalem** |

The High Sabbath of
The Feast of Unleavened Bread

The High Sabbath of the Feast of Unleavened Bread starts during the Passover meal at dusk, according to GOD's command in Exodus 12:16 A day with no work allowed except to prepare meals.

The Lord's first night and day in the tomb.

| 440 | 6ᵗʰ Day | Nisan 16 | **Jerusalem** |

**Feast Schedule
2nd day of Feast
of Unleavened Bread and First Fruits
The day of Preparation for the Weekly Sabbath
The Lord's second night and day in the tomb.**

| 441 | Sabbath | Nisan 17 | **Jerusalem** |

**Weekly Sabbath
Feast Schedule 3rd day of Feast
of Unleavened Bread and First Fruits
The Lord's third night and day in the tomb
and his Resurrection before sundown
ending the Sabbath.**

Week Sixty-Four
Year 28 AD

The last 5 days of the Feast of Unleavened Bread and First Fruits, ending in a High Sabbath, a day in which there is no work except for preparing meals.

| 442 | 1ˢᵗ Day | Nisan 18 | **Emmaus, Jerusalem** |

**First Fruits Offering
Feast Schedule 4th day of Unleavened Bread
First day of resurrection
The first day of the week, the High Priest makes the
First Fruits offering to GOD.**

John 20:14: At dawn, Mary and the women reach the tomb and Jesus is risen. When Mary sees and talks to

Jesus, he restrains her from touching him because he has not ascended to the Father.

Matthew 27:51 As He, Jesus, arose from the dead the holy ones that were resurrected after him, showed themselves to people in the city.

Luke 24:21 Jesus after ascending to the Father, appears to two disciples on the road to Emmaus and then appears to the disciples in Jerusalem and allows the eleven to touch him.

443	2nd Day	Nisan 19	**Jerusalem**

Feast Schedule 5th day of Unleavened Bread

444	3rd Day	Nisan 20	**Jerusalem**

Feast Schedule 6th day of Unleavened Bread

445	4th Day	Nisan 21	**Jerusalem**

Feast Schedule 7th day of the Unleavened Bread

446	5th Day	Nisan 22	**Jerusalem**

High Sabbath of the last day of Feast of Unleavened Bread

447	6th day	Nisan 23	**Jerusalem**
448	Sabbath	Nisan 24	**Jerusalem**

Week Sixty-Five
Year 28 AD

449	1st Day	Nisan 25	**Jerusalem**

Jn. 20:26-29

Jesus shows his scars to Thomas and Thomas believed

John: A week later, his disciples were in the house again, and Thomas was with them. Though the doors were locked Jesus came and stood with them and said "Peace be with you". Then he said to Thomas, "Put your finger here, see my hands reach out your hand and put it into my side, Stop doubting and believe." Thomas said to him, "My Lord and my GOD"!

450	2nd Day	Nisan 26	**Jerusalem**
451	3rd Day	Nisan 27	**Jerusalem**
452	4th Day	Nisan 28	**Jerusalem**
453	5th Day	Nisan 29	**Jerusalem**

Jn. 20:30-31

Jesus did many miraculous signs

John: Jesus did many other miraculous signs in the presence of his disciples, which are not recorded in this book. But these are written that you may believe, that Jesus is the Christ, the Son of GOD, and that by believing you might have life in his name.

454	6th Day	Iyyar 01	**Resurrection time**
455	Sabbath	Iyyar 02	**Resurrection time**

Week Sixty-Six
Year 28 AD

456	1st Day	Iyyar 03	**Resurrection time**

| 457 | 2nd Day | Iyyar 04 | **Resurrection time** |
| 458 | 3rd Day | Iyyar 05 | **Sea of Galilee** |

Jn. 21:1-15

Jesus cooks breakfast for the disciples

John: Jesus speaking, " Haven't you any fish?" No they answered, Jesus replies, "Throw your net on the right side of the boat and you will find some." When they did they were unable to haul the net in for the large number of fish. Then, the disciple that Jesus loved, said to Peter, "It is the Lord". ...Vs. 9 When they landed, they saw a fire of burning coals there with fish on it and some bread. Jesus said, "Bring some fish you have just caught". .... Jesus said to them, "Come have breakfast".

When they finished Jesus reinstated Peter.

459	4th Day	Iyyar 06	**Sea of Galilee**
460	5th Day	Iyyar 07	**Sea of Galilee**
461	6th Day	Iyyar 08	**Sea of Galilee**
462	Sabbath	Iyyar 09	**Sea of Galilee**

Week Sixty-Seven
Year 28 AD

463	1st Day	Iyyar 10	**Resurrection time**
464	2nd Day	Iyyar 11	**Resurrection time**
465	3rd Day	Iyyar 12	**Resurrection time**

466	4th Day	Iyyar 13	**Resurrection time**
467	5th Day	Iyyar 14	**Resurrection time**
468	6th Day	Iyyar 15	**Resurrection time**
469	Sabbath	Iyyar 16	**Resurrection time**

Week Sixty-Eight
Year 28 AD

470	1st Day	Iyyar 17	**By the Sea**
471	2nd Day	Iyyar 18	**By the Sea**
472	3rd Day	Iyyar 19	**By the Sea**
473	4th Day	Iyyar 20	**By the Sea**
474	5th Day	Iyyar 21	**Sea of Galilee**

Mt. 28:16-20   Mk. 16:15-18

Matthew: Meanwhile the eleven disciples set out for Galilee, to the mountain where Jesus had arranged to meet them. When they saw him they fell down before him, though some hesitated. Jesus came up and spoke to them, he said, "All authority in heaven and on earth has been given to me, Go, therefore, make disciples of all nations, baptize them in the name of the Father, the Son and the Holy Spirit.

| 475 | 6th Day | Iyyar 22 | **Sea of Galilee** |
| 476 | Sabbath | Iyyar 23 | **Sea of Galilee** |

Week Sixty-Nine
Year 28 AD

477	1st Day	Iyyar 24	**Resurrection time**
478	2nd Day	Iyyar 25	**Resurrection time**
479	3rd Day	Iyyar 26	**Resurrection time**
480	4th Day	Iyyar 27	**Resurrection time**
481	5th Day	Iyyar 28	**Near Bethany**

Mk. 16:19-20   Lk. 24:50-53

Day of the Lord's ascension into Heaven

Acts 1:9-12 After he said this he was taken up before their very eyes and a cloud hid him from their sight. They were looking intently up into the sky as he was going when suddenly two men dressed in white stood beside them, "Men of Galilee, they said why do you stand here looking into the sky? The same Jesus who has been taken from you into Heaven will come back in the same way you have seen him go into Heaven.

482	6th Day	Iyyar 30	**Jerusalem**

Lk. 24:51-53

The disciples stayed continuously at the Temple praising GOD

Luke: While he was blessing them he was taken up into heaven, vs.52 then they worshipped him and returned to Jerusalem with great joy. Vs.53 and they stayed continually at the temple Praising GOD.

| 483 | Sabbath | Sivan 01 | **Temple in Jerusalem** |

Week Seventy
Year 28 AD

484	1st Day	Sivan 02	**Temple in Jerusalem**
485	2nd Day	Sivan 03	**Temple in Jerusalem**
486	3rd Day	Sivan 04	**Temple in Jerusalem**
487	4th Day	Sivan 05	**Temple in Jerusalem**
488	5th Day	Sivan 06	**Temple in Jerusalem**
489	6th Day	Sivan 07	**Temple in Jerusalem**
490	Sabbath	Sivan 08	**Temple in Jerusalem**

Feast of Shavuots (Pentecost)

Feast Schedule 1st day of Pentecost

High Sabbath of Pentecost, 50th day of counting the Omer First day of the Feast of Shavuots (Pentecost) with required attendance at the Temple in Jerusalem. This Feast is centered around the Wheat harvest and the First Fruit offering.

Part Three

Introduction to Part Three

Parts One and Two establish the timing of the Ministry of Jesus Christ and its fulfillment of the Torah, the Prophets, and the Psalms.

Part Three deals with the specific timing of the Feast of Passover, Unleavened Bread and First Fruits and their interrelationship with the current celebration of Passion week and Easter. It is important to know the truth about the Feasts of GOD because Jesus Christ was living according to GOD's Feast schedule, not the Christian Holiday schedule.

Jesus, after resurrection, said to the two Disciples on the road to Emmaus after hearing their despair about Jesus not being the liberating king to the Jewish nation, Luke 24:25-26 "How foolish you are and slow of heart to believe all the Prophets have spoken. Did not the Christ have to suffer these things and then enter into his glory." And beginning with Moses and the Prophets, Jesus, explained to them what was said in all the scriptures concerning himself.

If The Messiah, Jesus Christ thought it important enough, on the day after his resurrection, to go through the Old Testament and point out all the prophecies and shadow pictures referring to himself to just two disciples. It needs to be important for us to see the plan of GOD and its fulfillment so that we might be instilled with faith for

GOD's future plan. There are about three hundred prophecies about Jesus Christ's "First Coming" but there are more than five hundred prophecies about the "Second Coming". Learning about the Feasts of GOD will confirm the first coming and give us a picture of the future coming of the Lord.

#4. There is biblical evidence
The Messiah, Jesus Christ
Followed God's chronology of the Feast of Passover, Unleavened Bread, and First Fruits.

The typical Christian view of the "Passion week" is triumphant entry on Palm Sunday, crucifixion on Good Friday, and resurrection on Easter morning at Sunrise. The Sacred Calendar, Jesus Christ was following, was centered on GOD's instruction for his Feast of Passover, Unleavened Bread, and First Fruits, not our celebration of Easter.

The structure and the timing of the Feasts start with GOD's instruction in Exodus: Exodus 12:2 Tell the whole community of Israel that on the tenth day of the month, each man is to take a lamb for his family, one for each household… vs.6 Take care of (lambs) them until the fourteenth day of the month, when all the people of the community of Israel must slaughter them at twilight….vs.8 That night they are to eat the meat roasted over the fire, along with bitter herbs and bread made without yeast…. v11 This is how you are to eat it: with your cloak tucked into your belt, your sandals on your feet and your staff in your hand, Eat it in haste, it is the Lord's Passover….v16 On the first day of the feast (Unleavened Bread) it shall be a High Sabbath and there shall be no work except to prepare food.

Detailed timing of the Month of the Abib (Nisan) and

Feasts of GOD. Exodus 23:15

The beginning of each day starts at the beginning of darkness in the evening.

9th Day is Rosh Hashanah the Head of the month and year starting with the sighting of the renewed moon in the month the barley is ripe. Exodus 12:1

10th Day of the Month The Passover Lamb is chosen and paraded to the Temple.

11th Day The family lambs and households are cleaned and washed

12th Day The children are taught about GOD's deliverance of Israel from slavery.

13th Day Prepare the table, clothes, each person, and the feast to await the lamb.

14th Day Passover Lamb is sacrificed at twilight and eaten with bitter herbs

15th Day The first day of the Feast of Unleavened Bread (High Sabbath)

16th Day The second day of the Feast of Unleavened Bread (Day of Preparation)

17th Day The third day of the Feast of Unleavened Bread (Weekly Sabbath)

18th Day The day of First Fruits offering.

19th Day Fifth day of the Feast of Unleavened Bread

20th Day Preparation for the High Sabbath ending First Fruits

21st Day The Last day (High Sabbath)

The Biblical narrative starts as Jesus Christ, the Messiah,

approaches Bethany on his way to Jerusalem for the Feasts of GOD. John 12:1. The scripture describes Jesus reaching Bethany two days before the beginning of 4 days of Feast preparation (or 6 days before Passover). Jesus probably arrived in Bethany in the afternoon of the 8th day of the month and the evening meal would have been the beginning of the 9th day.

Note: During Jesus Christ ministry the next day started at the sighting of three stars and followed with the night and day.

Daily detail of the days of preparation and the days of the Feasts of GOD

8th Day of the Month of Abib (Nisan) Jesus arrived in Bethany and met Lazarus, Mary, and Martha. John 12:1 Six days before the Passover, Jesus arrived at Bethany at the house of Lazarus. Jesus arrived in ample time for the 4 day preparation for the Passover feast as GOD has set out in Exodus 12:2. (Scripture above)

Luke 19:29 As they approached Bethany, Jesus sent two disciples saying "Go into the village ahead of you, as you enter it you will find a colt tied there, which no one has ever ridden, bring it here. If anyone ask you "why are you untying it"? Tell them the Lord needs it. Luke tells us (where John's Gospel did not) that the Lord rides the colt into town in the Triumphal Entry. Probably, the instruction to prepare the Passover in Luke 22:7 was more in the timing of getting the colt so they could meet the instructions of GOD in Exodus 12:2. To chose the Passover Lamb on the tenth day of the month.

9th Day of the month of Abib (Nisan) This is probably the day Jesus sent some disciples to Jerusalem to prepare the Passover which means:

Reserving a place for the 10th day of Nisan so that
- The live lamb can be chosen,
- Housed,
- Groomed and
- Live for four days.

The rooms must be cleaned and inspected for all leaven, with the last of the leaven burned on the fourteenth day of the month. Exodus 12.

Two of the Gospels have the Anointing of Jesus with perfumed oil on the first night after reaching Bethany and two Gospels have the anointing taking place on the third day of the week. The anointing is not a part of the timing of GOD for the Feast.

The preparation for the Feast of Passover, Unleavened Bread, and First Fruits starts at Nisan 10 and continues to Nisan 13.

Note (In 28AD the first day of preparation was on the Sabbath) movement and work on the Sabbath is prohibited except when the Sabbath is a preparation day of GOD's Feast. Movement and work is allowed, because it is a Divine Instruction required on a certain date, the 10th day of the month.

10th Day of the month of Abib (Nisan) 1st day of preparation for Passover and the day for choosing the Passover lamb for your family.

The High Priest goes to Bethlehem to choose the Passover Lamb for the nation, brings the lamb back to the streets filled with pilgrims with palm fronds and cedar boughs crowded into the streets of Jerusalem yelling "Hosanna, Blessed is he who comes in the name of the Lord, Hosanna, Peace in the Heavens and Glory in the highest. Hosanna, Blessed is he who comes in the name of the Lord, Blessed is the King of Israel"

This year Jesus Christ, Lord of the Sabbath, enters Jerusalem in triumph on a donkey's colt to the praises of the people in attendance to the Feasts on the tenth day of the Month on the Sabbath fulfilling Zechariah 9:9 & spoken of in Matthew 21:1-9 & John 12:12-16.

John 12:12 The next day the great crowd that had come for the feast, heard that Jesus was on his way to Jerusalem, they took out palm branches and went out to meet him shouting "Hosanna, Blessed is he who comes in the name of the Lord, Blessed is the King of Israel" (Psalm 118:25-27)

At the same time the crowd was waiting for the High Priest to return, with the Passover lamb to be sacrificed for Israel's sins, from Bethlehem and the High Priest enters after The Messiah. The High Priests was accompanied by a host of priests and Levites. Upon entrance to the city the pilgrims there for the feasts would shake their branches and shout "Hosanna, Blessed is he who comes in the name of the Lord, Blessed is the King of Israel" This had been done for over 1000 years.

11th, 12th, and 13th Day of the month (3 days of Preparation for Passover) All leaven is burned by the end of 14th the lamb is cleaned and groomed, and the household is cleaned, washed, and clothes darned. The children learn the story of Yahweh's deliverance of Israel from slavery in Egypt. They also, memorize prayers and questions to prompt more answers of GOD's deliverance and blessings for the Jewish nation.

Note: All four gospels give us a picture of the period leading up to Passover.

10th Day of the month is the Triumphal entry of Jesus, The Messiah to correspond with the High Priest bringing the perfect Passover lamb to the Temple to await inspection until Passover and

The cleansing of the Temple is the 11th day of Nisan and

12th Day starts with the withered fig tree and ends with the questioning of the Sadducees and Pharisees. As the plot thickens to kill Jesus (and Lazarus) Matthew in verse 26:2 announces there are two days left to Passover.

The last thing that happens during the four days of

preparation is the Last Supper.

14th Day of the month is Passover (also see Chapter 5 Last Supper was not Passover) The families sacrifice the Passover Lamb at twilight, roast it and eat it all with bitter herbs, unleavened bread and wine as found in Exodus 12. The high priest after sacrificing the last lamb informs the attendees "it is finished."

Then, after taking the lamb downstairs, under the Temple, to be roasted for the Passover Meal, the priest resurfaces to start the First Fruits offering process. The high priest with a large party of priests and attendees goes over to the Mount of Olives to bind together 10 shocks of Barley, to be harvested three days and three nights later after the weekly Sabbath. (The number of days is not always 3 days.)

GOD's timeline starts with the Passover followed by binding of the barley for the First Fruits offering, Passover meal followed by the High Sabbath of Unleavened Bread

15th Day of the Month. The High Sabbath of the Feast of Unleavened Bread starts in the midst of the Passover meal when the sundown is over.

This day is a High Sabbath, with no work except to prepare food, lasting until three stars are sighted the next afternoon/evening. Referred to in John 19:31 Since it was the day of Preparation, the Jews did not want the bodies left on the crosses during the Sabbath, especially because

that Sabbath was a day of great solemnity. (A High Sabbath)
It also is the beginning of the Lords entombment (day 1, night and day)

16th Day of the Month (also see chapter 6 on Good Friday)
Second day of the Feast of Unleavened Bread
Day of Preparation (commerce and work) for the Weekly Sabbath.
It is the second day of the Lord's entombment (day 2, night and day)

Note: The Post Temple Jews celebrate the First Fruits wave offering on the day after the High Sabbath of Unleavened Bread, but Jesus Christ and the Karaite Jews (Scripturalists) chose the day after the weekly Sabbath for the First Fruits offering.

A. The logic would fall with Jesus and the Karaite view because the counting of the omer would mimic the ripening of the barley with the ripening of the wheat but counting from the day after the High Sabbath of First Fruits will move as much as 6 days according to the day of the week without correlation to the growing process .

B. Since the instruction is to count the "omer" and the "seven Sabbaths", Pentecost is celebrated for seven days starting on the fiftieth day. One day after the seventh Sabbath. The only way the day after the seventh Sabbath can be the fiftieth day is to start with a Sabbath.

C. Also there are insinuations in the new testament that the Sabbath of Pentecost is followed by another Sabbath, Acts 20:7 This would indicate that Jesus and the Karaite view is correct.

D. The view of the First Fruits offering being the day after the High day of Unleavened Bread does not allow for the Resurrection to be three days and three nights after the crucifixion without contriving the Lord's words to mean two nights and three day parts all within 36 hours. Good Friday to Easter Sunrise.

E. Jesus followed the timing of the First Fruits Offering on the first day of the week as verified when Jesus said to Mary do not touch me for I have not yet ascended to my Father, later he returned and was touched by the Disciples.

F. Leviticus 23:15-17 tells us there are two ways of counting, fifty days, both days and weeks and celebrating the day of First Fruits offering on the day after the High Sabbath of Unleavened bread (the Pharisaical view) will only allow them to be correct, when the 16th of the month happens on the weekly Sabbath.

17th Day of the Month, Weekly Sabbath
(also See chapter 8 Resurrected on 3rd day)
Third day of the Feast
of Unleavened Bread and First Fruits
It is the third day in the Lord's entombment (3days and 3 nights and raised on the third day). This is the day of the

Lord's Resurrection, the Lord of the Sabbath is raised on the Sabbath three days and three nights after the crucifixion. At the same time the High Priest goes over to the Mount of Olives to harvest the First Fruits of the Barley to prepare for the offering at the morning prayers on the first day of the week.

As Jesus arose they arose, the resurrected saints came out of the graves and were seen in town by the inhabitants and the Priests harvesting the barley for their first Fruits offering were on the same Mount of Olives, where the cemetery was located.

18th Day of the Month,
First day of the week
(Also Chapter 9 First Fruits offering)
Fourth day of the Feast
of Unleavened Bread and First Fruits

Jesus Christ ascends to The Father and delivers the Holy ones resurrected with him as his First Fruits offering. Jesus is our High Priest and it was First Fruits.

Women appear at the tomb and find it empty
Beginning of the Resurrection 40 Day period
First Fruits offering of the barley harvest by the High Priest of the Jews
Jesus appears to two disciples on the road to Emmaus
See the information on First Fruits offering above on the 16th day of the Month.

19th Day of the Month,
Second day of the week
Fifth day of the Feast of Unleavened Bread
Second day of Resurrection period
20th Day of the Month,
Third day of the week
Sixth day of the Feast of Unleavened Bread
Third day of the Resurrection period
21st Day of the Month,
High Sabbath
Seventh Day of the Feast of Unleavened Bread
Fourth day of the Resurrection period.

Conclusion: "The Sacred schedule" of the Passion period of Jesus Christ, is based on GOD's schedule for "His" Feasts. The Lord, Jesus Christ, observed the commandments of GOD. It is important for us to know the truth and understand the Feasts of GOD. I am not here to try to change our Holidays but I am here to expose the incorrect timing of our Holidays that preclude the fulfillment of Biblical prophecies from being realized.

#5. What biblical evidence supports Jesus Christ, The Messiah's, Triumphal entry on Palm Sunday

The excitement of the Passion Week's triumphal entry was indescribable in the year 28 AD for several unusual reasons:

1. The Hebrew Nation had heard of Jesus doing two miracles that, no other person claiming to be the Messiah, had ever done: the raising of Lazarus from the dead after four days and the healing of a man born blind.

2. The Hebrew pilgrims in Jerusalem were tying to see the "King" they had been anticipating to redeem Israel.

3. Hundreds of thousands if not millions of Hebrew pilgrims were in Jerusalem to meet with their GOD and were lined up to welcome the High Priest as he brings the "Passover lamb" through the streets to be staked in the Temple for 4 days until Passover.

4. Parts of the Hebrew ruling body, teachers of the Torah, Pharisees, and Sadducees are seized with fear of losing their positions and power, and therefore plot to kill Jesus and Lazarus. Lazarus was a Pharisee and just being alive is a testimony to Jesus being the Messiah.

The problem with the timing of the Christian "Passion week of Jesus Christ" is that Jesus Christ, a Jew, is participating in GOD's Feast of Passover, Unleavened Bread, and the First Fruits offering not Easter.

The specific timing problems are:

1. The Triumphal entry must be on the 10th day of the month

2. The Passover & crucifixion must be on the 14th day of the month

3. The High Sabbath of Unleavened Bread must be on the 15th day of the month

4. First Fruits offering must be on the First Day of the week

5. The total number of days in the Feast Schedule is 8 days and in the Christian "Passion week" is seven days.

The second problem for "Christian Passion week timing" is having an annual year that starts with the sighting of the renewed moon on a day so that the Triumphal Entry can be on a Sunday or the First day of the week and having an eight-day week. Did you bring your calendar with you? GOD's schedule is exact and starts on the tenth day of the month, to prepare for His feasts.

Importance of the fulfillment of scripture instead of Jesus using his powers as GOD:

Example 1. Listen to Jesus speaking to Peter in Matthew 26:53 "Do you think I cannot call on my Father and he will at once put at my disposal twelve legions of angels. But how then will the Scriptures be fulfilled that say it must happen this way."

Example 2. And Jesus speaking to the two disciples on the road to Emmaus Luke 24:25, "How foolish you are, and how slow of heart to believe all that the prophets have spoken! Did not Christ have to suffer these things and then to enter his glory?" And beginning with Moses and all the Prophets he (Jesus) explained to them what was said in all the Scriptures concerning himself.

Example 3. Jesus speaking to the disciples about the great among you must be your servant Mark 10:45 said, "For even the Son of Man did not come to be served, but to serve, and to give his life as a ransom for many."

All three of these verses confirm, in our Lord's own words, that the timing and process of his life must happen as it has been prophesied and pictured in the Feasts of GOD.

Detailed timing of the Month of the Abib (Nisan) and the Feasts of GOD

The beginning of each day starts at the beginning of darkness in the evening.

1st Day is Rosh Hashanah the Head of the month and year starting with the sighting of the renewed moon in the month the barley is ripe. Exodus 12:1

10th Day of the Month The Passover Lamb is chosen and paraded to the Temple.

11th Day The lambs and households are cleaned and washed

12th Day The children are taught about GOD's deliverance of Israel from slavery.

13th Day Prepare the table, clothes, each person, and the feast to await the lamb.

14th Day Passover Lamb is sacrificed at twilight and eaten with bitter herbs

15th Day The first day of the Feast of Unleavened Bread (The High Sabbath)

16th Day The second day of the Feast of Unleavened Bread (Preparation Day for the weekly Sabbath.)

17th Day The third day of the Feast of Unleavened Bread (Weekly Sabbath)

18th Day The day of First Fruits offering.

19th Day Fifth day of the Feast of Unleavened Bread

20th Day Preparation for the High Sabbath ending First

Fruits
21st Day The Last day (High Sabbath)

There is no credible biblical evidence that the Triumphal entry was on Palm Sunday. Counting Backward from the Resurrection, which has to be prior to Mary's arrival at the tomb, before first light, on the first day of the week: Three days in the earth and raised on the third day therefore

17th Day of the month (Sabbath),
16th Day of the month,
15th Day High Sabbath of Unleavened Bread
14th Day Passover and Crucifixion at twilight
13th Day Last Supper at the ending of the day
Four days of preparation
13th Day of the month
12th Day of the month
11th Day of the month
10th Day (Sabbath) Triumphal Entry and choosing of the Passover Lamb
9th Day of the month
8th Day of Nisan (Abib)
Arrival in Bethany 6 days before Passover

The Christian "Passion week" is not founded on the timing of Passover and the Feast of Unleavened Bread and First Fruits and therefore GOD's sacred schedule of his Feasts Differs from the present day celebration in the following ways:

According to the Torah, there can only be four days between the triumphant entry and Crucifixion

In both testaments, there must be three days and three nights in the entombment period.

Jesus must be raised on the third day.

There must be a High Sabbath after Passover and before the weekly Sabbath to honor Exodus 12:2.

First Fruits offering must be made on the first day of the week.

11 Scriptural Reasons that the "Triumphal Entry" for the Christians and the parading of the Passover Lamb for the Jewish Nation happens on the Sabbath in the year 28AD on the tenth day of the month of the Abib (Nisan).

It does not need to be on a Sabbath it just happens on the Sabbath, but it must happen on the 10th day of the month.

#1. Exodus 12:2 Tell the whole community of Israel that on the tenth day of the month, each man is to take a lamb for his family, one for each household... v6 Take care of (lambs) them until the fourteenth day of the month, when all the people of the community of Israel must slaughter them at twilight....v8 That night they are to eat the meat roasted over the fire, along with bitter herbs and bread made without yeast.... v11 This is how you are to eat it: with your cloak tucked into your belt, your sandals on your feet and your staff in your hand, Eat it in haste, it is the Lord's Passover....v16 On the first day of the feast (Unleavened Bread) it shall be a High Sabbath and there shall be no work except to prepare food. This scripture lays out the exactness of GOD's schedule.

John 1: 29 the next day John "The Baptist" saw Jesus, "The Messiah" coming toward him and said, "Look the Lamb of GOD, who takes away the sin of the world." Every shadow picture of Jesus as the Lamb of God reinforces the image of Jesus being the Passover Lamb and therefore must enter Jerusalem on the same day as the other Passover lambs enter for the Feast.

#2. Luke 22:7 "Go and make preparation for us to eat the Passover" is out of time sequence if you are not familiar with the preparation for the Feast of Passover and Unleavened Bread. Exodus 12:2 lays out four days God has directed for preparation of the lamb and house hold from the 10th day through the 13th day of Nisan.

#3. John 12:1 six days before the Passover, Jesus arrived at Bethany at the house of Lazarus. Jesus arrived in ample time to prepare for the Passover feast as GOD has set out in Exodus 12:2. This timing fits with the necessary 4 days of preparation for Passover, the Feast of Unleavened Bread, and First Fruits.

#4. John 12:12 The next day the great crowd that had come for the feast, heard that Jesus was on his way to Jerusalem, they took out palm branches and went out to meet him shouting "Hosanna, Blessed is he who comes in the name of the Lord, Blessed is the King of Israel" Psalms 118:25-27

At the same time the (tenth day of the month), part of the crowd was waiting for the High Priest to return, with the Passover lamb to be sacrificed for Israel's sins, The high priest chose the lamb from Bethlehem. The High priest was accompanied by a host of priests, Levites, and pilgrims. Upon entrance to the city, the Hebrew pilgrims there for the feasts would shake their branches and shout "Hosanna, Blessed is he who comes in the name of the Lord, Blessed is the King of Israel"

Note A: Christ fulfilled each and every shadow picture of the feasts starting with the entrance of the Passover Lamb to the announcement of the people as to his real identity. GOD had this timing happen just as it has been rehearsed for more than a thousand years down to having Jesus Christ our Passover Lamb born in Bethlehem where all the "Passover" lambs were raised.

Note B: Father God is fulfilling his promise to Abraham and all of us who are the seed of Abraham. Abraham's prophecy, "GOD, himself, will provide the lamb for the burnt offering" Genesis 22:8

John 1:29 The next day John, the Baptist, saw Jesus coming toward him and said, "Look the Lamb of GOD, who takes away the sin of the world!"

#5. Luke 19:29 As they approached Bethany, Jesus sent two disciples saying "Go into the village ahead of you, as you enter it you will find a colt tied there, which no one has ever ridden, bring it here. If anyone ask you "why are you untying it? Tell them the Lord needs it." Luke tells us (where John did not) that the Lord rides the colt into town in the Triumphal Entry. Preparing to fulfill the prophecy of Zechariah 9:9.

The instruction to prepare the Passover in Luke 22:7 was more in the timing of the arrival into Bethany and getting the colt so they could meet the entrance instructions of GOD in Exodus 12:2. Preparation included choosing of a temporary home, choosing a spotless lamb for the sacrifice at Passover, cleansing of the Temple as well as the temporary home of the pilgrims, and would be "a work in progress" from the 10th to the 13th.

#6. Mark 11:1 tells us the same story of entering Bethany and sending the disciples for the colt. The timing in Mark tells us that the cleansing of the Temple was the day after the Triumphal Entry in verse Mark 11:12.

#7. Matthew 21:1 Matthew adds to the information of the other gospels by telling, " Go to the village ahead of you and at once you will find a donkey tied there, with her colt by her. Untie them and bring them to me.

Note C: All four gospels give us a picture of the period leading up to Passover. The 10th day of the month is the Triumphal entry, the cleansing of the Temple is the 11th day of Nisan and the 12th starts with the withered fig tree and ends with the questioning of the Sadducees and Pharisees. As the plot thickens to kill Jesus (and Lazarus) Matthew in verse 26:2 announces there are two days left to Passover, which matches the Feast calendar of four days preparation and then the Passover.

#8. Matthew 26:17 This verse is confusing without understanding that the translators added words to the scripture and there are four days of preparation before the Feasts.
(A) The words that the translators have added (Day and Feast)
(B) Passover and Unleavened Bread starts with four days of preparation.

On the first (day) of the (Feast of) Unleavened Bread, or without the added words, On the first of Unleavened Bread, the disciples came to Jesus and asked, "Where do you want us to make preparations for you to eat the Passover?" Jesus replied, Go into the city to a certain man and tell him. The Teacher says my appointed time is near. I am going to celebrate the Passover with my disciples at your house. If the scripture Matthew 26:17 "is as written" then Passover is over because Passover happens before the

Feast of Unleavened Bread and so the scripture must be translated incorrectly.

The purpose of this scripture is to inform us where the Last Supper will be held. The upper room at possibly John Marks family home. Probably the preparations were made around the time the master asked for the donkey.

#9. Mark 14:12 Again the translators added the words "the feast" and "lamb", And on the first day of (the Feast) of Unleavened Bread, when the Passover (lamb) was sacrificed his disciples said to him, "Where do you want us to go and prepare for you to eat the Passover". When you take out the added words, it reads, "And on the day of Unleavened Bread" the phraseology allows for the preparation days for the Feast according to Exodus 12:2.

There is a Fatal Error if you don't take out the added words and read it as the First day of Unleavened Bread, because that "day" is a High Sabbath of the Feast of Unleavened Bread and no work other than preparing the meal can be done and Passover is already complete which we know has not happened yet.

#10. Luke 22:7 Then came the day of Unleavened Bread upon which the Passover Lamb must be sacrificed. Jesus sent Peter and John saying, "Go and make preparation for us to eat the Passover". Where do you want us to prepare it? They asked. So that it reads "preparation for Unleavened Bread", in the sentence before, "they were reclining" for the last supper.

Had the disciples prepared "The Last Supper" for the Passover meal they would not have had leavened bread in the house, let alone, on the table for consumption against GOD's laws, not pharisaical law but GOD's law. The Greek word for bread here is (Artos) Leavened bread "And Jesus took bread" (artos) leavened bread is the same in all gospels that tell this experience.

Therefore this cannot be The High Sabbath of Unleavened Bread and be serving leavened bread but one of the days of preparation, because Jesus must be sacrificed on Passover, on the fourteenth day of the month and the Triumphal entry must be on the tenth day of Nisan, which in this year must be the weekly Sabbath and the Passover must be before the High Sabbath of Unleavened Bread.

11. Luke 23:54 And it was the day of preparation and the Sabbath was dawning (same Greek word as dusk…vs 55 The women who followed …saw the tomb and how he (Jesus) was laid. V56 Then they went home and prepared spices and perfumes. But they rested on the Sabbath in obedience to the commandment. 24:1 But on the first day of the week, at early dawn, they came to the tomb, taking the spices they had prepared.

Therefore because scripture says, that the Sabbath was beginning, and because the women were out of town, and commerce had quit about three o'clock before the Sabbath, probably they had not brought funereal perfumes and linen with them, they could not buy embalming materials until the day after the High Sabbath and then they bought and prepared spices and linen and waited through the weekly Sabbath, and came to the tomb on the first day of the week while it was still dark.

Conclusions

If the women rested on the Sabbath as the commandment said, then they rested on both Sabbaths of this week. So when did they prepare the spices? There must be a day between the High Sabbath and the weekly Sabbath. If there is a day between the two Sabbaths:

1. Can this timing work with the parameters set up by scripture? YES

2. Can Jesus be three days and three nights and raised on the third day? YES

3. Is the Choosing of the lamb 4 days from Passover? YES

4. Is there a non Sabbath day for the women to prepare the spices? YES

5. Is there a non Sabbath day for the Pharisees to ask Pilate for a guard? YES

6. Can the Last supper be the Last Supper and not be

The Seventy-Week Ministry, 178

Passover? YES

Schedule of The Feast of Passover, Unleavened Bread, and First Fruits and Passion weeks meeting the scripture requirements from GOD:

10th day of month	Sabbath	Triumphal Entry
11th day of month	1st of week	Preparation Day 2
12th day of month	2nd of week	Preparation Day 3
13th day of month	3rd of week	Preparation Day 4
14th day of month	4th of week	Passover, Cross, night in tomb
15th day of month	5th of week	High Sabbath
16th day of month	6th of week	Day 2 of the Feast
17th day of month	Sabbath	Weekly Sabbath
18th day of month	1st of week	Empty Tomb. Offering 1st Fruits.

Jesus ascends to the Father with the First Fruits offering and then comes back to see the disciples on the road to Emmaus hours later and in the evening appears to the disciples in the upper room.

#6. There is biblical evidence The Messiah, Jesus Christ Was at the Last Supper, but the Last Supper was not Passover.

Passover and The Last Supper are two different meals and have different and profound significance and power. The Passover Meal was GOD's protection of his chosen people from the "death angel" who was passing through the earth killing the first born in every household. GOD's deliverance at Passover had been celebrated and renewed every year since the exodus from Egypt. The Bread served at the Feasts being celebrated during the Passover and Unleavened Bread was "Azimos", Greek word for Unleavened Bread. The unleavened bread was made with piercing, stripes, and was charred.

The Last Supper is the Christian's covenant meal with GOD, celebrating the new covenant, not protecting us from the death angel but giving us eternal life through the substitution of Jesus Christ's right standing with GOD for our sin. The bread Jesus Christ served at this meal is a leavened bread (Greek word is "Artos") representing his body. Christ was wounded for our transgressions, bruised for our iniquities, and the stripes on his back were for our healing, but the bread served at the Last Supper was a full-bodied bread made with leaven.

Our new covenant does not require annual blood sacrifices to cover our sins, Romans 5:17 says it like this "For if by the trespass of the one man, death reigned through that one man, How much more will those who receive GOD's abundant provision of grace and of the gift of righteousness, reign in life through the one man, Jesus Christ".

GOD's schedule for his Feasts details the activities before the Feasts and the requirements of meals and activities after the Feasts start.

Fifteen Scriptural Reasons that the "Last Supper" is the "Last Supper" not Passover and the "Last Supper" happens before Passover and the High Day of Unleavened Bread. Because GOD said so!!!!, in his word starting in Exodus 12:2 Tell the whole community of Israel that on the tenth day of the month, each man is to take a lamb for his family, one for each household... v6 Take care of (lambs) them until the fourteenth day of the month, when all the people of the community of Israel must slaughter them at twilight....v8 That night they are to eat the meat roasted over the fire, along with bitter herbs and bread made without yeast.... v11 This is how you are to eat it: with your cloak tucked into your belt, your sandals on your feet and your staff in your hand, Eat it in haste, it is the Lord's Passover....v16 On the first day of the feast (Unleavened Bread) it shall be a High Sabbath and there shall be no work except to prepare food.

The Passover lamb is chosen on the 10th day of the month

and housed with the family until the 14th when it is sacrificed at twilight. Jesus was crucified just hours before the Passover meal, he was the fulfillment of GOD's Passover Lamb.

#1. Luke 22:7 "Go and make preparation for us to eat the Passover" is out of time sequence if you are not familiar with the four days to prepare the lamb and the household for the Feast of Passover and Unleavened Bread. Ex 12:2 lays out four days God has directed for preparation of the lamb and house hold from the 10th day through the 13th day of Nisan. Vs. Luke 22:14 when the hour came, Jesus and his Disciples reclined at the table....vs.15 Jesus said " I have eagerly desired to eat this Passover with you before I suffer....vs.16 For I tell you, I will not eat it (Passover) again until it finds fulfillment in the Kingdom of GOD." Jesus said he desired to eat Passover, but it does not say he did. Jesus also asked his Father to take this cup from him, but not my will but yours be done. (This didn't happen either.)

#2. Luke 22:14 When the hour came, Jesus and the apostles reclined at the table.
If this would have been Passover they would not have reclined, they would have been completely dressed and their cloaks tucked in their sandals on and their staffs ready and they would have eaten the meal in haste according to GOD's instruction in Exodus.

#2a. Luke 22:19 And he took bread (leavened bread

"artos") Serving leavened bread for the Passover meal would make everyone unclean for 7 days. Lev 12:8
Therefore it cannot be Passover meal with leavened bread
The Greek word here "Artos" is also the same word used for the leavened loaves that fed the 4,000 and the 5,000.

#3. Luke 22:38 The Disciples reported they had two swords and Jesus said that is enough.
Had this been after the Passover dinner, they could not have carried anything without it being considered work, because after the meal, when three stars are visible, it begins the High Sabbath of Unleavened Bread. At that time carrying two horsehairs was considered work because they could be made into a trap for birds, carrying more ink than necessary to draw two letters would be considered work.

#4. Luke 22:39 Jesus went out as usual to the Mount of Olives to the Garden of Gethsemane.
Had this been after the Passover meal which turned into The High Sabbath of Unleavened Bread with the sighting of three stars, it would begin a day of no work,
Jesus would not have entered into work. Ex 12:16

#5. Luke 22:47 Jesus Arrested ...vs.52 Then Jesus said to the chief priests.....
If the last Supper had been Passover the chief priests of the Jewish nation would not have been working because after Passover dinner it was a High Sabbath and they would have been defiled by being with the Roman Soldiers, also,

there cannot be any trials during the seven days of the Feasts.

#6. Luke 23:54 then he took down the body and wrapped it in linen cloth and placed it in a tomb...v 54 It was Preparation Day and the Sabbath was about to begin.
Luke announces to us that The Lord's death and burial happened on the Day of Preparation to the High Sabbath. Therefore the Last Supper certainly can't be on Passover.

#7. Mark 14:1 Now the Passover and the Feast of Unleavened Bread (Greek word for unleavened bread "Azymos") were only two days away, and the chief priests and the teachers of the law were looking for a sly way to arrest and kill him, but not during the Feast, they said or the people will riot.

Again, Any and all action with regard to arresting and killing Jesus had to be done before the Passover and the High Sabbath of Unleavened Bread. This certainly confirms that the Last Supper was on the day of preparation and not Passover.

#8. Mark 15:6 (Jesus before Pilate) Now it was the custom of Pilate, at the Feast, to release a prisoner whom the people requested ...v9 Do you want me to release to you the king of the Jews asked Pilate...v11 but the chief priests stirred up the crowd to have Pilate release Barabbas instead. arrest Jesus and kill him. The Passover has not happened because the Feast has not started.

#9. Mark 15:42 (The burial of Jesus) It was the Preparation day, that is the day before the (High Sabbath instead of weekly) Sabbath...v 46 So Joseph bought some linen cloth, took down the body, wrapped it in the linen, and placed it in a tomb cut out of rock. Had the Last Supper been Passover Joseph could not have bought Linen, because of the High Sabbath, which starts in the midst of the Passover Meal, allows no work but to prepare meals. The Sabbath after the day of Preparation must be the High Sabbath of the Feast and not the Preparation day of the weekly Sabbath because, once the Feast starts there can be no trials and no executions. This further illuminates that the Last Supper is before Passover Feast and meal begins.

#10. Matthew 27:62 (The guard at the tomb) The next day, the day after the day of Preparation. This gives a clear time line that not only was the Last Supper before Passover but the Lord was in the tomb before Passover and the Feast of Unleavened Bread.

#11. John 18:28 Then the Jews led Jesus from Caiphas home to the palace of the Roman governor. By now it was early morning and to avoid ceremonial uncleanness the Jews did not enter the palace: for they wanted to eat the Passover.

This adds to the timeline that confirms that the Last Supper was not Passover, but the Last Supper.

#12. John 19:13 When Pilate heard this, he brought Jesus

out and sat down on the judges seat…..vs.14 It was the day of Preparation of Passover about the Sixth hour. He is your king.

Another confirmation that the Last Supper was before the Passover meal begins.

#13. John 19:31 Now it was the day of Preparation and the next day was to be a special Sabbath. Because the Jews did not want the bodies left on the crosses during the Sabbath, they asked Pilate to have the legs broken and the bodies taken down. Exodus 12:16 On the first day of the feast it shall be a High Sabbath and there shall be no work except to prepare the meals.

This verse has special significance because it not only announces that this day is a day of preparation for Passover but also highlights that the next day is a High Sabbath of the Feast of Unleavened Bread.

#14. Luke 23:55 The women who followed …saw the tomb and how he (Jesus) was laid. V56 Then they went home and prepared spices and perfumes. But they rested on the Sabbath in obedience to the commandment.

The women would not have had to rest on the next day because it would not be the Sabbath but V54 tells us It was Preparation Day and the Sabbath was about to begin.

Another sign that the Last Supper is on the day of

preparation to the Feast of Passover.

#15. John 13:29 (while at the Last Supper) Since Judas had charge of the money, some (disciples) thought Jesus was telling Judas to buy something for the feast or to give something to the poor. V 30 As soon as Judas had taken the bread, he went out. And it was night.

This is a DYNAMIC PROOF that the Last Supper was not Passover because the Disciples thought that Judas leaving the Last Supper, after the foot washing, was sent by Jesus to buy something for the Feast. Had the Feast started you can't buy anything!

If you believe that the Last Supper was Passover then you must deal with the following sins of the Savior you say you follow:

#1. Jesus serving Leavened Bread (Artos) at the Last Supper and defiling the entire group and being in opposition to GOD and his Laws for the Feast of Passover.

#2. The Passover meal would have been served on the wrong day of the month and wrong day of week and would be against the Plan of GOD.

#3. The high priest would not have marked the first fruits shocks of barley for the First Fruits offering and be out of timing with GOD's instruction concerning Feasts and First Fruits offerings.

#4. There is not one hint that lamb, bitters, four cups of wine, a place set for Elijah, the Story of deliverance from slavery in Egypt told, questions from the children and many other details of the Passover meal were completed at the Last Supper.

#5. The Lord would have been disobeying GOD's commands to not work when he (1) washed the Disciples feet and he would have been disobeying GOD (2) when he told the disciples to carry two swords on the High Sabbath,

#6. The High Priest, Pharisees and Sanhedrin, all would have been working on the High Sabbath of the Feast of Unleavened Bread. After a thousand years of following GOD's directives, this year the "Jews" decided to celebrate on a different day than GOD required.

#7. There can be no arrests, trials, executions, or burials during any feast of Yahweh without uncleanness for whoever had to deal with the dead body. These are not the Feast of the Jews "They are the Feast of GOD" The Feasts are GOD's appointed time to meet with his people, not a time for his people to meet with their GOD.

#8. Jesus would not have sent Judas out to buy something for the feast if the Feast of GOD had started.

Conclusion: Scripture does not support the Last Supper being the Passover meal. The Last Supper is our covenant meal given to us by Jesus Christ in order to remember his sacrifice in body and blood.

What biblical evidence Supports, The Messiah, Jesus Christ being Crucified on Good Friday?

If you believe in the Triumphant Entry being on Palm Sunday, then Passover and the crucifixion have to be on Thursday four days after the choosing and parading of the Passover Lamb. If you are not convinced by Exodus 12:2 and still believe in Crucifixion on Good Friday then you must deal with the fatal errors to the time sequence allowing the Crucifixion followed by the Weekly Sabbath. In the end, there is NO credible evidence that Jesus was crucified on Friday. (the 6th day of the week)

If the Crucifixion is followed by the Weekly Sabbath, The prophecy of "three days and three nights and raised on the third day" is not true. (There are only 36 hours From Friday evening to dawn on Sunday morning). Jesus Christ did not say three-day parts, no matter how hard people want to sell you their agenda, Jesus did not need to bend or shade the truth. If Jesus said, three days and three nights and raised on the third day, then that is what he meant, or he could of said I will be raised in 36 hours.

If the Crucifixion is followed by the Weekly Sabbath, Then there is no High Sabbath of the Feast of Unleavened Bread therefore the entire Jewish community is acting against GOD's instructions and the scripture in John 19:31 announcing that the next day was the High Sabbath of

Unleavened bread.

If the Crucifixion is followed by the weekly Sabbath then Jesus did not arrive in Bethany 6 days prior to Passover.

If the Crucifixion is followed by the weekly Sabbath then there is not a day with the freedom for the Pharisees and Teachers of the Law to go to Pilate to request a guard for the tomb because Jesus had said he would rise again on the third day. Matthew 27:62

If the Crucifixion is followed by the weekly Sabbath then there is not a day with the freedom for the women to buy and work to prepare the perfumes and oils for proper burial for Jesus.

Note: Before answering the "one on one" questions the larger question is What calendar can be used to base the dating of Passover being on a Friday and in what year does that calendar say the Crucifixion happened on a Friday? Was Jesus Christ using the same calendar to schedule his attendance to the Feast of GOD? How old was Jesus at the Resurrection and how does that correlate with all the timing points in Luke and the prophetic requirements of our Savior and High Priest. These are questions that point out just some of the problems of dating things of GOD.

No Matter what Calendar you are using GOD requires the feast be celebrated according to a "His" schedule for Passover, Feast of Unleavened Bread, and First Fruits.

After the new moon beginning the month of Nisan (Aviv or Abib) GOD's schedule must have a day for each part of the Feast, and the Last Supper is an event Jesus added.

GOD Requirements
Year 28AD

10th day of month	Sabbath	Preparation Day 1. Lamb chosen
11th day of month	1st day of week	Preparation Day 2
12th day of month	2nd day of week	Preparation Day 3
13th day of month	3rd day of week	Preparation Day 4. Last Supper
14th day of month	4th day of week	Passover Sacrifice and meal
15th day of month	5th day of week	High Sabbath of Unleavened Bread
16th day of month	6th day of week	Preparation for weekly Sabbath
17th day of month	Sabbath	Resurrection
18th day of month	1st day of week	First Fruits Offering

Each one of these Feast days is spoken of in the gospels, and the Old Testament confirms that this is the correct order.

The obvious fatal error in contemporary Passion Week timing is the absence of the High Sabbath of Unleavened bread. The Lord was crucified at the same time as the other Passover Lambs were being sacrificed, but current theology skips the High Sabbath of Unleavened Bread and goes right to the weekly Sabbath in spite of all the instructions of Exodus 12:2 and 12:16 and John 19:31.

Twelve Scriptures that detail the trial, crucifixion, and burial were complete before Passover and the High Sabbath of Unleavened Bread and two days before the Weekly Sabbath.

#1. Exodus 12:2 Tell the whole community of Israel that on the tenth day of the month, each man is to take a lamb for his family, one for each household… vs.6 Take care of (lambs) them until the fourteenth day of the month, when all the people of the community of Israel must slaughter them at twilight….vs.8 That night they are to eat the meat roasted over the fire, along with bitter herbs and bread made without yeast…. Vs.11 This is how you are to eat it: with your cloak tucked into your belt, your sandals on your feet and your staff in your hand, Eat it in haste, : it is the Lord's Passover….vs.16 On the first day of the feast (Unleavened Bread) it shall be a High Sabbath and there shall be no work except to prepare food.

Note: This gives us GOD's timeline which puts the Passover followed by the High Sabbath then a day of work, and the weekly Sabbath. This timing could not be accurate if the crucifixion was followed by the weekly Sabbath.

Also, there are four days of preparation before Passover and there can be up to six days of preparation before the weekly Sabbath.

#2. Luke 23:54 Then he took down the body and wrapped it in linen cloth and placed it in a tomb...vs.54 It was Preparation Day and the Sabbath was about to begin.

Note: Luke announces to us that The Lord's death and burial happened on the Day of Preparation to the Sabbath. If this Sabbath is the Weekly Sabbath instead of the High Sabbath then both Sabbaths must be on the same day and John 19:31 negates this idea because it refers to the Passover Meal and High Sabbath of Unleavened Bread to begin quickly.

#3. Mark 14:1 Now the Passover and the Feast of Unleavened Bread were only two days away, and the chief priests and the teachers of the law were looking for a sly way to arrest Jesus and kill him, but not during the Feast, they said or the people will riot.

Note: Any and all action with regard to arresting and killing Jesus had to be done before Passover and Unleavened Bread because the High Priest and other priests cannot be working, conducting trials, burying bodies, etc. on the High Sabbath or at any time after the feast has begun.

#4. Mark 15:42 (The burial of Jesus) It was the Preparation day, that is the day before the Sabbath…v46 So Joseph bought some linen cloth, took down the body, wrapped it in the linen, and placed it in a tomb cut out of rock.

Note: Had this been the High Sabbath of Unleavened Bread instead of the day the Passover is sacrificed: Joseph could not have bought Linen. This Sabbath indicated as the next day must be the High Sabbath of the Feast of Unleavened Bread and not the Preparation day of the weekly Sabbath because, Once the Feast starts there can be no trials and no executions. This further illustrates that the burial is before the Passover meal and Feast begins.

#5. Matthew 27:62 (The guard at the tomb) The next day, the day after the day of Preparation, the chief priests and Pharisees gathered before Pilate and said "Sir, we remember that the impostor said while he was still alive, after three days I will rise again."

Note: This scripture gives a clear time line that the trial, crucifixion, and burial was before Passover meal and the High Sabbath of the Feast of Unleavened Bread.
(1) Because it is talking about the guards at Jesus tomb.
(2) Had the day after the day of preparation been the High Sabbath of Unleavened Bread or Weekly Sabbath the

priests could not have been speaking to the Romans, for that would render them unclean.
(3) The day after the day of preparation has to be the High Sabbath of Unleavened Bread or the Weekly Sabbath, but the way this reads is "The next day, the day after the day of Preparation": this shows that the second day in the Tomb is the day when work and commerce could be accomplished.

#6. John 18:28 Then the Jews led Jesus from Caiaphas home to the palace of the Roman governor. By now it was early morning and to avoid ceremonial uncleanness the Jews did not enter the palace: for they wanted to eat the Passover.

This adds to the timeline that confirms that the Last Supper and the trial was before Passover and the High Sabbath of Unleavened Bread.

#7. John 19:13 When Pilate heard this, he brought Jesus out and sat down on the judges seat…..vs.14 It was the day of Preparation of the Passover about the Sixth hour. He is your king.

Another confirmation that Jesus Trial was on the day of preparation of Passover and Jesus would be dead by Sundown.
(1) The trial was well before the Passover Feast began, not only does it mention it was earlier but the Jews made Pilate come outside because they would be defiled if they

went into the home of a gentile and they would not be able to eat the Passover meal.

(2) Also this Preparation day is linked in the Greek to being the preparation day of Passover about the 6th hour.

(3) This clearly is not the day of preparation for the weekly Sabbath but preparation for the Passover meal, which goes into the High Sabbath of Unleavened Bread after three stars are visible.

#8. John 19:31 Now it was the day of Preparation and the next day was to be a SPECIAL Sabbath. Because the Jews did not want the bodies left on the crosses during the Sabbath, they asked Pilate to have the legs broken and the bodies taken down… when the soldiers came to Jesus they did not break his legs because he was already dead, instead one of the soldiers pierced his side with a spear bringing a sudden flow of blood and water.

VERY IMPORTANT TIMELINE because it tells us that the day after the day of preparation was a special Sabbath. The High Sabbath of the Feast of Unleavened Bread not the weekly Sabbath.

#9. John 19:38 Later Joseph of Arimathea, asked Pilate for the body of Jesus….Taking Jesus body, Joseph and Nicodemus wrapped it in spices and strips of linen. ..This was in accordance with Jewish customs….Because it was the Day of Preparation and since the tomb was nearby they laid Jesus there. There cant be any dead bodies left on a cross during the Feast. Joseph and Nicodemus were both

Pharisees and members of the Sanhedrin who had become disciples of Jesus Christ, The Messiah. Joseph and Nicodemus entire life had been wrapped up in obeying the law, in this case making sure Jesus was buried before the Passover meal and the High day of Unleavened Bread began.

#10 John 13:29 (while at the Last Supper) Since Judas had charge of the money, some (disciples) thought Jesus was telling Judas to buy something for the feast or to give something to the poor. V 30 As soon as Judas had taken the bread he went out. And it was night.

This is a DYNAMIC PROOF that the Last Supper was after sundown and the Disciples thought that Judas leaving the Last Supper, after the foot washing, was sent by Jesus to buy something for the Feast. It is important to note that it is night and therefore in Jewish reckoning of time the next day, if it had been the Passover meal, the feast would have begun and there could not have been commerce by Judas. Also the Trial, crucifixion, and burial could not start after the start of Passover Feast. Both of these proofs point out timing of the Last Supper, the trial, crucifixion, and burial were all before the Passover Feast.

#11. Jesus on the road to Emmaus Luke 24:21.... Are you only a visitor to Jerusalem and do not know the things, that have happened there in these days. Vs.19 Jesus asked them "What things?' they replied, The things about Jesus of Nazareth who was a Prophet mighty in deed and word before GOD and all the people, Vs.20 and how our chief priests and leaders handed him over to be condemned to death and crucified him.

Note 1: It is the third day since all this took place…. Then Jesus said to them, "How foolish you are and how slow of heart to believe all that the prophets have spoken! Vs.26 did not the Christ have to suffer these things and then enter his glory." And beginning with Moses and the Prophets he explained to them what was said in all the scriptures concerning himself.

Note 2: the notification by the Disciples that there had been three days since the happenings in Jerusalem destroys all timelines of the current Easter weekend. Since they are talking on the fourth day and they remark that there are three complete days since these things transpired. Since this is the first day of the week then the crucifixion and burial happened before the Passover meal.

#12. Mark 15:6 (Jesus before Pilate) Now it was the custom at the Feast for the Governor to release a prisoner whom the people requested …v9 "Do you want me to release to you the king of the Jews". asked Pilate…v11 but the chief priests stirred up the crowd to have Pilate release Barabbas instead.

Passover had not yet started. Therefore Jesus Christ cannot be crucified on Good Friday the day before the weekly Sabbath because scripture would be in contradiction to itself on many different levels.

What biblical evidence Supports, The Messiah, Jesus Christ being Resurrected on Easter Sunday?

Understanding GOD's reckoning of time, starts with the timing of the "day". When Jesus Christ was in Jerusalem the "day" began in the evening and followed with the night and day, from Genesis 1. This knowledge will help us determine the days of the entombment of Jesus Christ and the timing and fulfillment of the Resurrection prophecies. We cannot use our reckoning of time, or the Gregorian calendar, which is less than 500 years old to date things of GOD two thousand years ago.

The Sacred Calendar starts in Genesis where GOD sets the sun, moon, and stars in the heavens for the marking of the days, weeks, months, years and Feasts of GOD. The computer has given mankind the information necessary to reconstruct GOD's calendar,

(1) Exodus 13:4 the first month of the year starts on the sighting of the new moon in the month that the Barley crop is Abib (Ripe within the month). Hebrew name Rosh Hashanah, the head of the year.

(2) Any year that the Barley is not ripe (Aviv) a thirteenth month of Adar is added to the prior year. A thirteenth month is referred to as Veadar or Adar II

(3) In this way GOD, eliminated mans need for written record by basing the calendar on the moon and the growing season with a self correcting mechanism to adjust the years to the cycle of the earth around the sun and the moon around the earth.

In Exodus 12:1 GOD gives the timing of his Feasts, Passover, Unleavened Bread, and First Fruits (Talking about Passover) Yahweh said to Moses and Aaron in Egypt, This month must be the first of all months for you, the first month of your year.
Exodus 12:2 Tell the whole community of Israel that on the tenth day of the month, each man is to take a lamb for his family, one for each household
Vs.6 Take care of (lambs) them until the fourteenth day of the month, when all the people of the community of Israel must slaughter them at twilight....
Vs.8 That night they are to eat the meat roasted over the fire, along with bitter herbs and bread made without yeast....
Vs.11 This is how you are to eat it: with your cloak tucked into your belt, your sandals on your feet and your staff in your hand, Eat it in haste, it is the Lord's Passover....
Vs.16 On the first day of the feast it shall be a High Sabbath and there shall be no work except to prepare food.
Further information comes in Exodus 34:18 you will observe the Feast of Unleavened Bread. For seven days you will eat unleavened bread, as I have commanded you, at the appointed time in the month of Aviv, for in the month of the Aviv you came out of Egypt.

Should the "Lord of the Sabbath" be resurrected on the first day of the week or should our Savior be offering a First Fruits offering on offering day of GOD's Feast in the Heavenly Temple, as Hebrews says about Jesus," one who has become a High Priest
> not on the basis of regulation as to his ancestry
> but on the basis of the power of an indestructible life
> for it is declared:

"You are a Priest forever, in the order of Melchizedek." Hebrews 7:16-17

Understanding the beginning of the "calendar day" at twilight was difficult as you can see in the translation of the word "Sabbaton"

There are sixty-five references in the New Testament for the word "sabbaton". They are divided into 60 translations to "Sabbath" and the five references to "first day of the week". The five references are all describing the arrival at the tomb by Mary and the other women on the first day of the week.

There is no credible biblical evidence that The Messiah, Jesus Christ, is resurrected on Sunday the first day of the week.

Then Jesus said to them (Mark 2:27), "The Sabbath was made for man, not man for the Sabbath. So the Son of Man is Lord even of the Sabbath." After the Resurrection in Luke 24:46 Jesus told the Disciples (10 gathered in the upper room) "The son of man must be delivered into the hands of sinful man, be crucified, and on the third day be raised again" Then they remembered his words.

Our lack of knowledge of the Feasts of GOD and in this case the Feast of First Fruits keep us from seeing Jesus Christ as our High Priest with the importance that GOD required of the High Priests and his duties. In the early Jewish times, The High Priest is held in seclusion below the Temple to make sure that he did not defile himself between Passover sacrifice and Marking the ten shocks of barley and the First Fruits harvesting at the end of the weekly Sabbath.

The High priest sins must be covered so that GOD will accept his First Fruits Offering.

Jesus Christ, our High Priest, doesn't have to be kept in seclusion so he wont sin because he is a Priest after the Order of Melchizedek and is sitting on the right hand of The Father in Heaven, on our behalf.

These scriptures from Hebrews highlight the need to understand the Feasts of GOD and the duties of the priest. Jesus, our Messiah, was not through when he was crucified, nor when he was resurrected, but he was finished with the first three Feasts of GOD when he made the First Fruits offering on the first day of the week.

Hebrews 9:21 This is the blood of the covenant that GOD

has ordained for you, and in the same way he (Moses) sprinkled with the blood both the tent and the vessels used in worship, vs. 22 Indeed under the law almost everything is purified with blood, and without the shedding of blood there is no forgiveness of sins.

Hebrews 9:23 Therefore it was necessary for the patterns of the heavenly things to be purified with these rites, but the heavenly things need better sacrifices than these. For Christ did not enter a sanctuary made with human hands, a mere copy of the true one but he entered into heaven itself, now to appear in the presence of GOD in our behalf.

The Women arriving at dawn at the empty tomb, but Jesus Christ was risen.

All four of the Gospels say that Mary and the other women reached the tomb early in the morning and Jesus was not in the tomb, "very early on the first day of the week", Mark in 16:2

Towards the dawn of the first day of the week, Mary and the women reach the sepulcher There was a violent earthquake, for an angel of the Lord, descending from Heaven came and rolled away the stone and sat on it ....The angel spoke to the women, there is no need for you to be afraid ....he (Jesus) is risen just as he told you. Come and see the place where he lay. Matthew 28:1

On the first day of the week, at the first sign of dawn, they brought the spices they had prepared. They found the stone rolled away, but when they entered, they could not find the body of the Lord Jesus. Luke 24:1

It was very early on the first day of the week and still dark when Mary came to the tomb and saw that it was empty John 20:1

Note 1:
The tomb was empty "before" the earthquake and the angel welcoming the women to see the place where he laid. All the expressions in the Matthew account of the resurrection of Jesus Christ are in the past tense, signifying that Jesus was resurrected before they got to the tomb. Jesus did not need the angel or an earthquake to move the stone so he could exit. The earthquake and the angels were there to roll away the stone from the tomb so everyone coming to the tomb could see the empty tomb and know Jesus Christ was risen. Not one scenario from the Gospels has definitive timing on the resurrection of Jesus Christ: it only tells that Jesus was raised before the women reached the tomb before dawn on the first day of the week. The actions of the High Priest and the First Fruits offering show us the exact timing. The First Fruits harvesting which happens three days and three nights after the Passover sacrifice give us the timing of the fulfillment of the shadow picture of GOD's Feast of First Fruits.

Note 2:
The word translated "first day of the week" in the above

four references and in Mark 16:9 is translated as "Sabbath" in sixty other scriptures in the New Testament. Also the word "day" has been added by the Translators and the word for "dusk and dawn" are the same word in Greek.

There is one direct mention of the resurrection on first day of the week in the longer version of Mark, which is in contradiction to itself. According to all four Gospels the women arrived at the tomb at the dawn and he (Jesus) was not in the tomb but later in the longer version of Mark 16:9 It is announced "Jesus having risen early in the morning of the first day of the week, he appeared first to Mary. This being in contradiction to verse Mark 16:1-7.

If you read or punctuate the verse "Jesus having risen, (comma or period) Early in the morning of the first day of the week appeared first to Mary". This reading of the verse does not contradict itself with verse Mark 16:1-7

Here are Eight Scriptures that set up a substantial framework and demonstrate there are three days and three nights and raised on the third day, from the Crucifixion to the resurrection.

1. After the Resurrection, Luke 24:46 Jesus speaking to the Disciples in the upper room says, "The Son of Man must be delivered into the hands of sinful man, be crucified, and on the third day be raised again". Then they remembered his words."

Dynamic proof: If the ladies arrived at the tomb before dawn and Jesus was crucified at twilight on Friday, it is impossible for our celebration of the three days and three nights and raised on the third day to be correct in any interpretation of the Lord's words. Not three days, not three nights, and not raised on the third day: do you think the Lord has it wrong or do you think we have it wrong?

2. Matthew 27:63 the next day, the one after the Preparation Day, the chief priests and the Pharisees went to Pilate. Sir, they said, "we remember while he was still alive that deceiver said" "After three days I will rise again" So give the order for the tomb to be made secure until the third day.

3. Matthew 12:38 ...we want a sign...Jesus answered, A wicked and adulterous generation ask for a miraculous sign. But none will be given it except the sign of the Prophet Jonah. For as Jonah was three days and three nights in the belly of a great fish, so the Son of Man will be three days and three nights in the heart of the earth. Vs.41 the men of Nineveh will stand up at the judgment with this generation and condemn it: for they repented at the preaching of Jonah and now one greater than Jonah is here.

4. Mark 8:31 Jesus then began to teach them that the Son of Man must suffer many things and be rejected by the elders, chief priests, and teachers of the law and that he must be killed and after three days rise again.

5. Mark 10:33 We are going up to Jerusalem, Jesus said, and the Son of Man will be betrayed to the chief priests and teachers of the law. They will condemn him to death and hand him over to the gentiles, who will mock him and spit on him, flog him and kill him. Three days later he will rise.

6. Luke 24:20 The chief priests and our rulers handed him over to be sentenced to death, and they crucified him, but we had hoped that he was the one that would redeem Israel. And what is more it is the third day since all this took place. Looking forward Theologians explain away the three days and nights by saying that there were three day parts and the Jews used inclusive reckoning of time, but looking backwards at time exposes the failure of there theory, as is the case in this scripture.

7. On the road to Emmaus Luke 24:21....It is the third day since all this took place....Then Jesus said to them, "How foolish you are and how slow of heart to believe all that the prophets have spoken! Vs.26 did not the Christ have to suffer these things and then enter his glory." And beginning with Moses and the prophets he explained to them what was said in all the scriptures concerning himself.

8. 1st Corinthians 15:4 For what I have received I pass on to you, of first importance that Christ died for our sins, according to the scriptures, that he was buried, that he was raised on the third day according to the scriptures, and that

he appeared to Peter and then to the twelve.

Conclusion: The Hebrew reckoning of time, with the night and day starting at dusk and ending at dusk, allows three nights and three days to pass and for Jesus to be raised on the third day. This timing fits precisely with all scripture and Hebrew tradition of the Feast of First Fruits.

First Fruits is on the First day of the week
Jesus had not ascended with the resurrected saints and would not let Mary touch him, because he had not ascended to his Father.

Another indication that First Fruits offering is on the first day of the week, is that the counting of the Omer can't be done correctly without the Day of Pentecost being on the first day of the week. Leviticus 23:15-16 (Counting the weeks and the Omer) And ye shall count unto you from the morrow after the Sabbath from the day that ye brought the sheaf of the wave offering: seven Sabbaths shall be complete: Seven unto the morrow after the seventh Sabbath shall ye number fifty days: and ye shall offer a new meat offering unto Yahweh.

The First Fruits offering is offered on the day after the weekly Sabbath instead of the day after the High Sabbath of Unleavened Bread. The fulfillment of the Feast of First Fruits explains why Mary was not allowed to touch Jesus, until Jesus had ascended to his Father, with the Saints that had been resurrected and the repentant thief. Then Jesus returned to meet the two disciples on the road to Emmaus and later met the disciples in the upper room and let them touch him.

Establishing that Pentecost is seven Sabbaths and one day proves the High Sabbath of Pentecost is always on the First day of the week.

Acts 20:7 And upon the first day of the week, when the disciples came together to break bread, Paul preached….

This day is Pentecost because (1) the disciples are all together on the first day of the week (normally a work day except at Pentecost) when 50th day after the seventh weekly Sabbath is the High Sabbath of Pentecost (Shavuots).

Another proof, In the Greek interlinear, "And on one of the Sabbaths having been assembled us to break bread Paul was lecturing them"

Notice that the Sabbaths are plural (2) Acts 20:16 Paul had decided to sail past Ephesus, to avoid spending time in Asia, for he was in a hurry to reach Jerusalem, if possible, by the day of Pentecost. This would indicate as half of the Jewish Scholars, also believe, that the day of the First Fruits offering is the day after the weekly Sabbath and would line up with Jesus resurrection being on the end of the weekly Sabbath, after three days and three nights, from the even between Passover and High Sabbath of

Unleavened Bread to the weekly Sabbath.

For all these reasons and scriptures it is evident that the Lord of the Sabbath was not Resurrected on the first day of the week, the following verses are negative reasons Jesus Christ was not raised on Easter Sunday.

Fourteen Fatal Errors you believe for Jesus to be raised on Easter Sunday

John 19:31 now it was the day of Preparation and the next day was to be a special Sabbath. Because the Jews did not want the bodies left on the crosses during the Sabbath, they asked Pilate to have the legs broken and the bodies taken down.

Exodus 12:16 On the first day of the feast it shall be a High Sabbath and there shall be no work except to prepare the meal.

The first fatal error you have to believe is that there was not a High Sabbath this year as called for by GOD and identified above in John 19:31 for the first day of Unleavened Bread, the only date possible would be Friday, which is the day of preparation and Friday (6th day of the week) was definitely not a day of rest and therefore Jesus could not be raised on the 1st day of the week.

Matthew 12:38 …we want to see a miraculous sign from you. Jesus answered, "A wicked and perverse generation asks for a miraculous sign. But none will be given except for the sign of the Prophet Jonah. For as Jonah was three days and three nights in the belly of a huge fish, so the Son of Man will be three days and three nights in the heart of the earth.

The 2nd fatal error you have to believe is that Jesus did not mean what he said more than four times "he would be in the heart of the earth three days and three nights" and repeated many more times by other people who heard Jesus say the previous prophecy.

Exodus 12:2 Tell the whole community of Israel that on the tenth day of the month, each man is to take a lamb for his family, one for each household… vs.6 Take care of (lambs) them until the fourteenth day of the month, when all the people of the community of Israel must slaughter them at twilight….vs.8 That night they are to eat the meat roasted over the fire, along with bitter herbs and bread made without yeast…. Vs.11 This is how you are to eat it: with your cloak tucked into your belt, your sandals on your feet and your staff in your hand, Eat it in haste, it is the Lord's Passover….vs.16 On the first day of the feast it shall be a High Sabbath and there shall be no work except to prepare food.

The third fatal error you have to believe is that Passover is on sixth day of the week on the day of preparation. This is not possible because there are at least 10 verses that say this is "the day of preparation" which is always before Passover because after Passover the Feasts has begun. There is no appropriate day for their to be a High Sabbath of Unleavened Bread as talked about in John 19 and Exodus 12:16.

The fourth fatal error you have to believe is that there are four days between the triumphal entry and Good Friday. According to Exodus 12:2, there are four days between the entry and the Sacrifice, if the Passover is on the Friday or Saturday. This is a fatal error.

The fifth fatal error you have to believe is that the choosing of the Passover lamb did not happen on the 10th day of the month (which was the previous Sabbath) and the Passover was on the 14th, and what ever day you pick, it is not after 4 days after, as required by GOD in Exodus 12:2-16.

The sixth, seventh, eighth and ninth fatal errors that you have to believe is that Jesus, after telling us that he would fulfill all the old testament prophecies and shadow pictures of the feasts, that (6th) he was not the "lamb chosen from the beginning of time and triumphed in his entry to Passover on the 10th day of the month and (7th) not the Passover Lamb Sacrificed at twilight on the 14th and (8th) not the Messiah who rose again after three days and nights, and (9th) not raised on the Sabbath because he is not the Lord of the Sabbath.

The tenth, fatal error that you have to believe is that (10) the marking of the First Fruits of the Barley happens before the Passover when it is written that the barley shocks are marked for harvest after the last Passover Lamb is sacrificed and before the Passover meal begins.

The Eleventh fatal error to the Passover being on Friday (6th day of the week) or Saturday (the 7th day of the week) When Jesus reaches Bethany it says that it was 6 days to Passover and it indicates the next day or day after, to be the Sabbath.

Belief that he road the colt into Jerusalem on the Sunday for the Triumphal Entry means Passover has to be on the 4th or 5th day of the week, which makes Sunday, or the First day of the week a fatal error.

The twelfth fatal error you have to believe is that the two men on the way to Emmaus lied about it being three days since the Lords Crucifixion.

After the Resurrection, Luke 24:46 Jesus speaking to the Disciples in the upper room Says, "The Son of Man must be delivered into the hands of sinful man, be crucified, and on the third day be raised again". Then they remembered his words."

The thirteenth and fourteenth fatal errors are that Jesus did not tell the truth when he said three days and three nights and raised on the third day to the disciples and The disciples were delusional when they remembered Jesus saying he would be in the earth three days and three nights and raised on the third day.

Conclusion: Any belief that the present schedule of the Lord being crucified on Good Friday and being raised at sunrise on Easter is a farce and cannot be backed up by credible evidence.

Let us pray and act in love about celebrating Easter, the word in the Bible translated Easter is Pesach which is the Greek word for Passover. When people changed the name, the timing, and the custom of the Feasts of Yahweh to fit there own agenda, the changes were accepted by Christianity, and we followed our leaders and today we are still following: days of the week, months of the year, and our religious feasts named or timed for sun god worship. GOD warned us against these things in Exodus 34:11 Covenant given by GOD as they are entering "The Promised Land"

> …Take care you make no pact with the inhabitants of the land which you are about to enter, or they will prove a snare in your community. You will tear down their altars, smash their cultic stones and cut down their sacred poles for you will worship no other god, since Yahweh's name is the Jealous One: he is a jealous GOD, Make no pact with the inhabitants of the country or when they prostitute themselves to their own gods and sacrifices to them they will invite you and you will partake of

their sacrifice, and then you will chose wives for your sons from their daughters, and their daughters prostituting themselves to their own gods will induce your sons to prostitute themselves to their gods. You will not cast metal gods for yourself.

Conclusion: The Lord was crucified on Passover and raised three days later on the weekly Sabbath, just as he said. The Greek word for Passover is "Pascha or Pesach" and should not be translated "Easter" it was and is and always will be a poor representation of the fulfillment of the Passover Feast, crucifixion and resurrection of our Lord.

There is biblical evidence
The Messiah, Jesus Christ
Fulfilled the prophecy of Jonah
and was resurrected on the third day.

Timing of the Resurrection,
Which scriptures help us determine the duration of The Lord's entombment?

What fatal errors do you have to believe to have Jesus buried on Good Friday and raised on Easter Sunday? How did "easter" (Acts 12:4) the bare breasted Babylonian fertility god get in my Bible. The Greek word translated easter is "Pesach" Passover/ Unleavened Bread not easter.

Problems with Greek Translators
telling us about Jewish Feasts

In 325 A.D., The council of Nicea, with good intentions, set the celebration of Easter, to replace Passover, as the first Sunday after the new moon after March 21 (the spring solstice) but before April 25. Think about it, can you remember one scripture setting up new Feasts, or moving the Sabbath to a new day.

Constantine, after his supposed change to Christianity united his nation into one religion and setting up the day of worship on the day they worshipped the sun "Sunday". The current Christian movement decided to move "the Sabbath day" to the day assumed to be the day of the resurrection, the first day of the week. The Non Jewish Christians did not have training in the Feasts and instructions of Yahweh. Most of the new converts to Christianity had never been to Jerusalem and had no knowledge of the Old Testament. Therefore "we" have grown up with very little knowledge of the Feasts of GOD and therefore we have been indoctrinated into Holidays chosen by people who were not well versed in the instructions of GOD as to our Jewish Heritage, but instead they grew up in cultures worshiping false gods of sun, fertility and many others.

Jesus, The Messiah, never did away with any of the Torah. Jesus, only added "the sacraments of the Bread and the Wine to commemorate his death, burial, and resurrection and the new covenant."

It is important to remember that:
    Jesus was Jewish,
    the Apostles were Jewish,
    the people being taught were Jewish,
    the people being healed were Jewish. (With a few exceptions)
    the miracles were happening to the Jews
    the great commission was given to Jews
    the early converts were Jewish and that the term Christian comes into use in Antioch 15 years after Jesus is crucified.

Questions that need to be resolved
1."Does three days and three nights and raised on the third day", really mean what the Lord said, or can we make it

work, so that it all happens on one weekend so we can be back at work on Monday?

2. How does the timing of Passover, High Sabbath of Unleavened Bread, weekly Sabbath, and First Fruits offering help us determine the timing of Jesus Christ fulfillment of prophecy and each Feast?

15 Scriptures that illustrate how many times the Lord told the disciples, the Jewish leadership, and later the disciples told Christians that Jesus was going to be in the tomb three days and three nights and rise again on the third day. And 6 Scriptures that are after the resurrection that validate the timing of "three days and three nights and raised on the third day".

The most repeated prophecy describing the entombment timing in the Bible is the "three days and three nights"

#1.Jonah 1:17 But the Lord provided a great fish to swallow Jonah, and Jonah was inside the fish three days and three nights.

#2. Matthew 12:38 …(Pharisees) we want to see a miraculous sign from you. Jesus answered, "A wicked and perverse generation asks for a miraculous sign. But none will be given except for the sign of the Prophet Jonah. For as Jonah was three days and three nights in the belly of a huge fish, so the Son of Man will be three days and three nights in the heart of the earth.

#3. Matthew 16:4 The Pharisees and Sadducees came to Jesus and tested him by asking him to show them a sign from Heaven. Jesus replied…A wicked and adulterous generation looks for a miraculous sign, but none will be given it except the sign of the prophet Jonah.

#4. Matthew 17:22 (Jesus speaking) The Son of Man is going to be betrayed into the hands of men. They will kill him, and on the third day he will be raised to life.

#5. Luke 11:29 As the crowds increased, Jesus said, "This is a wicked generation. It asked for a miraculous sign, but none will be given it except the sign of Jonah, for as Jonah was a sign to the Ninevites, so the Son of Man will be to his generation".

#6. Matthew 27:63 The next day, the one after the Preparation Day, the chief priests and the Pharisees went to Pilate. Sir, they said we remember while he was still alive that deceiver said" After three days I will rise again" So give the order for the tomb to be made secure until the third day.

#7. Matthew 12:38 …we want a sign…Jesus answered, A wicked and adulterous generation ask for a miraculous sign. But none will be given it except the sign of the Prophet Jonah. For as Jonah was three days and three nights in the belly of a great fish, so the Son of Man will be three days and three nights in the heart of the earth. V41 The men of Nineveh will stand up at the judgment with this generation and condemn it: for they repented at the preaching of Jonah and now one greater than Jonah is here.

#8. Mark 8:31 Jesus then began to teach them that the Son of Man must suffer many things and be rejected by the elders, chief priests, and teachers of the law and that he must be killed and after three days rise again.

#9. Mark 10:33 we are going up to Jerusalem, Jesus said, and the Son of Man will be betrayed to the chief priests and teachers of the law. They will condemn him to death and hand him over to the gentiles, who will mock him and spit on him, flog him and kill him. Three days later he will rise.

#10. Mark 14:58 we heard him say, I will destroy this man made temple and in three days will build another, not made by man. Yet even there statements did not agree. (During the trial at Caiaphas house)

#11. John 2:19 Jesus answered them, Destroy this temple, and I will raise it again in three days....vs. 24 but the body Jesus spoke of was his body.

#12. Matthew 26:61 pointing to Jesus this fellow said, I am able to destroy the Temple of GOD and rebuild it in three days (witness in trial)

#13. Luke 24:7 The Son of Man must be delivered into the hands of sinful men, be crucified and on the third day be raised again.

#14 Luke 24:46 He told them, this is what is written: The Christ will suffer and rise from the dead on the third day.

#15. Luke 24:20 (Talking to the two Disciples on the road to Emmaus) the chief priests and our rulers handed him over to be sentenced to death, and they crucified him, but we had hoped that he was the one that would redeem Israel. And what is more it is the third day since all this took place.

Six scriptures after the resurrection that point out Jesus was three days and three nights in the Tomb.

#1. On the road to Emmaus Luke 24:21....It is the third day since all this took place....Then Jesus said to them, "How foolish you are and how slow of heart to believe all that the prophets have spoken! V26 did not the Christ have to suffer these things and then enter his glory." And beginning with Moses and the prophets he explained to them what was said in all the scriptures concerning himself.

#2. Acts 20:7 And upon the first day of the week, when the disciples came together to break bread, Paul preached... I believe this day is High Sabbath of Pentecost because (1) The disciples are all together on the first day of the week (normally a work day except at Pentecost) when 50th day after the seventh weekly Sabbath is the High Sabbath of

Pentecost (Shavuots) (2) Luke 20:16 Paul had decided to sail past Ephesus, to avoid spending time in Asia, for he was in a hurry to reach Jerusalem, if possible, by the day of Pentecost.

Therefore: This would indicate as half of the Jewish Scholars, also believe, that the day of the First Fruits offering is the day after the weekly Sabbath and would line up with Jesus resurrection after three days and three nights, in time for Jesus to make the First Fruits wave offering by taking the Holy ones who were resurrected with him to the Father when he ascended.

#3. The belief that Jesus was raised on the first day of the week is based on two ideas:
A. Mary and the women "Very early on the first day of the week when it was still dark." Went to the tomb. He was risen. The only fact we know from their arrival and Jesus being risen is that the resurrection happened before dawn on the first day of the week.
B. Translators also don't mention the significance of the First Fruits offering which is made on the morning after the weekly Sabbath and is connected to the morning when Jesus said to Mary, "don't touch me I have not yet ascended to My Father"

The women's schedule to prepare spices, linen, and ointments gives a picture of both Sabbaths and the Lords resurrection being three days and three nights.

#4. And when the Sabbath (High Sabbath of Unleavened Bread) was over, Mary Magdalene, Mary the Mother of Jesus and Salome bought spices, so they might anoint the body of Jesus. Mark 16:1

Luke 23:55 It was the day of preparation and the Sabbath was beginning. The women who had come with him from Galilee followed, and they saw the tomb and how his body was laid. Then they returned and prepared spices and on the Sabbath they rested according to the commandment.

Notice (A) In Luke, The Sabbath was beginning: the women would not have been able to work on or buy spices and ointments because the Passover meal was starting and during that meal when three stars were visible the High Sabbath of Unleavened Bread began.

(B) The women who had followed Jesus from Galilee, would not have had spices with them, and therefore would have waited through the High Sabbath to the day of preparation for the Weekly Sabbath, then bought and prepared the spices and if they finished preparing the spices they could go to the tomb or wait through the weekly Sabbath to the first day of the week to go to the tomb.

And Mark 16:1 agrees with this timing "After High Sabbath on the day of preparation for the weekly Sabbath spices bought and prepared, then resting on the weekly Sabbath, and going to the tomb very early on the first day of the week. Note: The women may have tried to go to the tomb on the 6th day of the week and the Roman Soldiers told to come back after three days on the first day of the week.

#5. Mark 16:1
And when the Sabbath was over (High Sabbath). Mary Magdalene, Mary the Mother of James and Salome bought spices so they might go anoint him. (They did not buy spices before dawn on the first day of the week)

Verse 1 is a stand-alone sentence. It indicates the High Sabbath of Unleavened Bread was over: the spices were purchased on the preparation day before the Weekly Sabbath
Verse 2: Very early on the first day of the week, just after sunrise they were on their way to the tomb and they ask each other who will roll the stone away from the front of the tomb? When you look at verse 2 it is two days after Verse 1 because "bought" indicates a day of commerce and work because they "bought and prepared" spices and the Sabbath would have had no work or commerce. Therefore it is two days before the first day of the week, because they arrived at the tomb before dawn on the first day of the week.

The conclusion: A. When you combine the timing from Mark 16:1 announcing the Sabbath was over before they bought the spices, but announcing it was before dawn. Therefore there must be a day of commerce when the women bought the spices.

B. Luke 23:55 Announcing that the Sabbath was beginning (If the Sabbath is beginning they cant buy spices until there is a day of commerce.) and that the women left and returned to buy and prepare the spices and then rested on the Sabbath Making the first Sabbath the High Sabbath of Unleavened Bread then a day of Commerce then the weekly Sabbath. This is one more proof of the fulfillment of the Prophecy of Jonah and the Lord Jesus Christ that he was in the earth for three days and raised on the third day.

#6. 1 Corinthians 15:4 Paul confirms in his writing and says it is of first importance. For what I received I passed on to you as of first importance that Christ died for our sins according to the scriptures that he was buried that he was raised on the third day.

Thirteen fatal errors you have to believe to have the Messiah crucified Friday evening and raised on Sunday Morning.

There are only two nights and two days from Friday night to Sunday morning, 36 hours from Friday at 6:00 in the evening to 6:00 Sunday morning.

John 19:31 Now it was the day of Preparation and the next day was to be a special Sabbath. Because the Jews did not want the bodies left on the crosses during the Sabbath, they asked Pilate to have the legs broken and the bodies taken down.

Exodus 12:16 On the first day of the feast it shall be a High Sabbath and there shall be no work except to prepare the meal.

The first fatal error you have to believe is that there was not a High Sabbath called for by GOD, for the first day of Unleavened Bread, the only date possible would be Friday, which is the day of preparation and Friday (6th day of the week) was definitely not a day of rest.

Matthew 12:38 ...we want to see a miraculous sign from you. Jesus answered, "A wicked and perverse generation asks for a miraculous sign. But none will be given except for the sign of the Prophet Jonah. For as Jonah was three days and three nights in the belly of a huge fish, so the Son of Man will be three days and three nights in the heart of the earth.

The 2nd fatal error you have to believe is that Jesus did not mean what he said more than four times "he would be in the heart of the earth three days and three nights" and repeated many more times by other people who heard Jesus say the words.

Exodus 12:2 Tell the whole community of Israel that on the tenth day of the month, each man is to take a lamb for his family, one for each household... vs.6 Take care of (lambs) them until the fourteenth day of the month, when all the people of the community of Israel must slaughter them at twilight…. vs.8 That night they are to eat the meat roasted over the fire, along with bitter herbs and bread made without yeast…. Vs.11 This is how you are to eat it: with your cloak tucked into your belt, your sandals on your feet and your staff in your hand, Eat it in haste, : it is the Lord's Passover….vs.16 On the first day of the feast it shall be a High Sabbath and there shall be no work except to prepare food.

The third fatal error you have to believe is that Passover is on the sixth day of the week. This is not possible because there is no appropriate day for their to be a High Sabbath as talked about in John 19 and Exodus 12:16.

The fourth fatal error you have to believe is that the Passover is not four days from the triumphal entry and the choosing of the Passover Lamb according to Exodus 12:2 and there are not four days between the triumphal entry and the Sacrifice, if the Passover is on the Friday or Saturday.

The fifth, sixth, seventh, eighth and ninth fatal errors that you have to believe that Jesus, after telling us that he would fulfill all the old testament and feasts, that (5th error) he (Jesus) was not the "lamb chosen from the beginning of time and (6th) did not triumph in his entry to Passover on the 10th day of the month and (7th) not the Passover Lamb Sacrificed at twilight on the 14th and (8th) not the Messiah who rose again after three days and nights, and (9th) not raised on the Sabbath because he is not the Lord of the Sabbath.

The tenth fatal error that you have to believe is that (10) the marking of the First Fruits of the Barley happens before the Passover when it is written that the barley shocks are marked for harvest after the last Passover Lamb is sacrificed and before the Passover meal begins.

The eleventh fatal error to the Passover being on Friday (6th day of the week) or Saturday (the 7th day of the week) When Jesus reaches Bethany it says that it was 6 days to Passover and it indicates the next day or day after, that he road the colt into Jerusalem on the Sabbath for the Triumphal Entry. That means Passover has to be on the 4th or 5th day of the week, which makes Friday a fatal error.
The twelfth fatal error you have to believe is that the two men Jesus appeared to on the way to Emmaus lied about it being three days since the Lords Crucifixion.

The thirteenth fatal error you have to believe is that the information Jesus gave to Paul, was a lie, in 1 Corinthians 15:3 For what I received I passed on to you as of first importance that Christ died for our sins according to the scriptures, that he was buried and that he was raised on the third day, according to the scriptures.

Conclusion, The Lord was crucified on the fourth day of the week and was resurrected on the Sabbath and ascended to the Father with the first offering as our High Priest on the first day of the week. In these events Jesus Christ fulfilled the prophecies and shadow pictures of the spring feasts of GOD.

There is biblical evidence
The Messiah, Jesus Christ
Fulfilled the First Fruits offering
As has been pictured for 1,000 years.

Fulfillment of the Old Testament offering requirements and actions of the High Priest will reveal and help us to understand the Lord's First Fruits offering to GOD as our High Priest. Their actions will reveal timing of the Passion weeks of the Messiah, Jesus Christ.

Duties of Jesus Christ, our High Priest, a priest after the order of Melchizedec.

The Messiah, Jesus Christ, is our new High Priest, after the order of Melchizedek, who sat down at the right hand of the throne of the Majesty in heaven and who serves in the sanctuary, the true tabernacle set up by the Lord, not by man. Hebrews 8:1b

Hebrews starting at chapter 7 and going through chapter 10 explores the duties of the High Priest and the new covenant. Hebrews 9:23 Therefore it was necessary for the patterns of the heavenly things to be purified with these rites (the blood), but the heavenly things need better sacrifices (blood of Jesus) than these. For Christ did not enter a sanctuary made with human hands, a mere copy of the true one but he entered into heaven itself, now to appear in the presence of GOD in our behalf

Respect for the Torah and the Prophets

Matthew 4:17 Jesus speaking, do not think that I have come to abolish the Law (Torah) and the Prophets, I have not come to abolish them but to fulfill them. I tell you the truth, until heaven and earth disappear, not the smallest letter not the least stroke of a pen, will by any means disappear from the law until everything is accomplished. The shadow pictures set up by GOD Almighty when he setup His Feasts are as important as the prophecies we expect the Lord to fulfill from the Prophets.

Warnings of "adding to" or "taking away" from the Bible
Revelation 22:18 I warn everyone who hears the words of the prophecy of this book. If any one adds anything to them, GOD will add to him the plagues described in this book. And if any one takes words away from this book of prophecy. GOD will take away from him his share of the Tree of Life and in the Holy City, which are described in this book.

To learn about the fulfillment of GOD's Feast of Passover and First Fruits, we must examine what the High Priest of the Jewish nation was doing during the Feast, because it will be a shadow picture of the Lord's fulfillment.

As the last Passover Lamb is sacrificed the High Priest yells out, "it is finished"
Priesthood duties in the service of the First Fruits Offering start with the sacrifice of the last Passover lamb.

There are two parts to the First Fruits offering

(1) The marking of the First Fruits of the barley. The priests marked the first fruits of the barley by tying (not cutting) ten shocks of barley together right after the last Passover Lamb is sacrificed and minutes before the High Sabbath of Unleavened bread starts. The barley grown, for this purpose, was on the side of the Mount of Olives. The High priest, after he marked the First Fruits of the Barley, was kept in seclusion under the Temple, for three days and three nights and resurfaced on the third day for the harvesting of the barley for the offering of the First Fruits on the First Day of the week. This seclusion was to insure that he would not do anything that would defile his sanctification from the Passover sacrifice until after he had offered the First Fruits offering.

At the end of the Weekly Sabbath

(2) The harvesting and preparing of the barley. The Priests harvest the ten shocks of Barley, after the evening of the Weekly Sabbath, so that they can be prepared for the wave offering as the First Fruits of the Barley along with a spotless lamb of the first year, to GOD in the Temple, on the morning of the first day of the week.

The actions of Jesus Christ, our High Priest Follow the pattern of the High Priest for the First Fruits offering.

As Jesus Christ prepared to give up his life on the cross he said "it is finished"

Then the marking of the First Fruits began
(The Holy Ones graves opened)
Matthew 27:51 ... The veil of the Sanctuary was torn in two from top to bottom, the earth quaked, the rocks were split, (1) THE TOMBS OPENED and the bodies of many holy people rose from the dead, The cemetery was also on the Mount of Olives.

The Harvesting of the First Fruits
(2) AND THESE (Resurrected Saints), AFTER HIS RESURRECTION, came out of the tombs, entered the holy city and appeared to a number of people. At the same time as the priests are harvesting the barley and from the same Mount of Olives where the resurrected saints are coming out of the tombs.

For Jesus, our new High Priest
(1) Jesus marked the tombs by opening them: notice they were not harvested until he arose. To expand the truth of Jesus and the First Fruits offering, the pivotal point in this scripture, is the timing of the opening of the graves (at Jesus death) and

(2) Three days later, resurrection of these Holy ones (at Jesus resurrection) Specifically the scripture says: And these after his resurrection came out of the tombs entered the Holy City and appeared to a number of people.

At this time the High Priest of Israel has harvested the barley and prepared it for the wave offering along with a spotless lamb of the first year at the morning sacrifice of First Fruits. This sacrifice is made on the morning of the first day of the week.

The First Fruits offering is the answer
to why Mary could not touch Jesus in John 20:14 and Thomas could touch him in John 20:26

If you said Jesus was male chauvinists, you would be wrong. The key is that Jesus Christ, acting as our High Priest, had not ascended to the Father with his First Fruits offering. Ask yourself what happened to the Holy ones who arose when he arose? John 20:14...Jesus said "Mary!" She turned around then and said to him in Hebrew, Rabbani!" Which means Master. Jesus said to her. Do not touch me, because I have NOT YET ASCENDED TO MY FATHER. Later that same day (one gospel says this is a week later) Jesus returned, after ascending to the Father, to the upper room where the disciples were gathered and let Thomas touch Him. John 20:26.... Jesus came and stood among them and said " Peace be with you" then he said to Thomas, "Put your fingers here and see my hands: reach out your hand and put it in my side".

If Jesus Christ was crucified wearing only a girdle and left his grave clothes in the Tomb then where and what was he wearing when Mary saw him and did not recognize him. I believe the angels brought him 4 white linen garments that the High Priest has to wear to make the First Fruits offering of the barley and the spotless lamb of the first year. This is another reason that Mary could not touch Jesus Christ until he had made the First Fruits offering.

It was a scary thing not to obey the Pharisee rules and GOD's laws
When you study the period of time of Jesus ministry, the Jewish society was held together by 613 rules, instructions GOD put in the Torah. The Priests and Jewish leaders added man made rules that brought condemnation for virtually every person: the society was not built on "Grace" but instead laws, guilt, and sacrifice. Notice that the conversations between Jesus and the Teachers of the Torah, Pharisees, and Sanhedrin usually contained this phrase from Mark 7:9 Jesus speaking," You have a fine way of setting aside the commandment of GOD in order to observe your own traditions."

To Understand the Jewish First Fruits offering
And the First fruits offering of Jesus Christ our High Priest You must understand the resurrections mentioned in the Bible.

The Apostle Paul tells us there are three resurrections in 1Corinthians 15:22.
Jesus Christ is our new High Priest, after the order of Melchizedec: He is definitely the only High priest that can offer the First Fruits Offering in the Heavenly Tabernacle.

The repentant thief on the cross and "the Holy saints" resurrected when Jesus was resurrected were part of the

First Fruits offering.

When studied 1 Corinthians 15:22 puts in order the three Resurrections:
1st First Fruits, 1st / 2nd Christ, 3rd at Christ coming.
It is not "Christ the First Fruits". There were no punctuations in the original text and the word "the" was not in the original. It should read the resurrections are:
    Christ,
    First Fruits, and
    Christ's at his coming.

Christ is first born from the Dead, Revelation 1:5 Grace and peace to you, who is, who was, and who is to come. Christ is "First born from the dead", but not the first fruits wave offering to GOD. Jesus Christ waved the first fruits offering and was in himself the blood of the Lamb of the first year, presented to his Father in the Heavenly Temple where Christ operates as our High Priest.

The New Revised Standard (Resurrections)
1 Corinthians 15:22 ...Just as all die in Adam, so in Christ all will be brought to life, BUT ALL IN THEIR PROPER ORDER: Christ, (the) First Fruits, and next, at his coming, those who belong to him. After that will come the end. "The" was added and was not in the original text.

The New Greek Interlinear (Resurrections)
1 Corinthians 15:22 For as in Adam all die, so also in Christ all will be made alive, BUT EACH ONE IN HIS

OWN ORDER: (the) First Fruits, Christ, afterward the ones of Christ in the coming of him, then the end. When he gives over the Kingdom to GOD even (the) Father, when he abolishes all rule and all authority and power.

Conclusion: Look at the shadow picture Yahweh gave the Israelites of the First Fruits offering and believe Jesus is our High Priest and is "The One" presenting the "Holy ones that were resurrected" to the Father in the real Holy of Holies and then returning to meet the two disciples on the road to Emmaus. This scenario would answer the questions:
1. What happened to the resurrected Holy ones if they did not go to Heaven with the Lord?
2. Why could Mary not touch the risen Lord and Thomas could several hours later?
3. Why were the graves opened at crucifixion and Holy ones resurrected at the Lord's resurrection three days later?
4. If it does not happen as this scenario portrays, then how are the Feasts of Passover, Unleavened Bread, and First Fruits going to be fulfilled?

A Daily look at the feast days from Passover through the First Fruits offering on the first day of the week.

14th day of the month – Passover
(1) The priest as he prepared to sacrifice the Passover lambs said "I find no fault in him" and then the sacrifice is made. Pilate and Herod said many times of Jesus "I find no fault in him"

(1a) Jesus crucifixion and death happened at the same time, as the Jewish families sacrifice the Passover Lamb at twilight and roast it and eat it with bitter herbs, and unleavened bread.

(2) The high priest after sacrificing the last lamb informs the attendees "it is finished"
(2a) Jesus after completing his task on the cross says "It is Finished"
The picture of the Lords Crucifixion is a picture of our Passover Lamb.

(3) (Jesus is being put in the earthen tomb) The high Priest, after taking the Passover lamb downstairs under the Temple, to be roasted for the Passover Meal, the High Priest resurfaces and with a large party of priests and attendees goes over to the Mount of Olives to bind together 10 shocks of Barley. Then the High Priest stays in seclusion for three days and three nights until the First Fruits are harvested at the end of the Sabbath to prepare the barley for the wave offering on the first day of the week.
(3a) At Jesus death, the earth quaked and the tombs on the Mount of Olives were opened and marked. Then Jesus was in the tomb three days and three nights until his resurrection at the end of the Sabbath and the Holy ones in the graves were resurrected and showed themselves to people in the city.

Nisan 15, High Sabbath of Unleavened Bread

Nisan 16, Preparation day,
Nisan 17, Weekly Sabbath
Three nights and three days later

Nisan 17, Right after the sunset on the Sabbath
(4) First Fruits of the barley to be harvested, after the weekly Sabbath, by the High Priest, priests and attendees. They assemble on the Mount of Olives to watch the harvesting and to prepare the barley for the Wave Offering. On the morning at first prayers the barley is offered to the Lord.

(4a) (Jesus harvests the tombs of the Holy ones on the Mount of Olives) As he was resurrected, they (Holy ones in the tombs) were resurrected and were seen by hundreds in the city (and all the priests and attendees watching the harvesting of the barley). Another shadow picture to fulfill the First Fruits offering.

(5)While the priests and the attendees were harvesting the barley,
(5a) the Lord is resurrected and the Saints come out of the graves on the same mount where they are harvesting the barley. Can you imagine the sight to the priests and pilgrims there for the First Fruits harvest of the barley? When the priests are offering their wave offering of the First Fruits of the barley, the Lord, our High Priest, was in the Heavenly Temple with his First Fruits offering.

Nisan 18, First day of the week at morning Prayers

(6) Day of the First Fruits wave offering
Priests prepare barley through the night for the First Fruits offering on the morning of the First day of the week.

(6a) Jesus meets Mary and won't let her touch him (John 20:14) because he has not yet ascended to his Father. Not allowing Mary to touch Him does not make since unless you are familiar with First Fruits offering because Jesus allows Thomas to touch him later (John 20:26). Jesus is about to take the Resurrected saints, to his Father and the Heavenly Temple as his first fruits offering (see 1Corinthians 15:21-22) at the same time the priests are offering the first fruits of the barley in the earthly Temple of GOD. Jesus is back in hours to meet the disciples on the road to Emmaus.

If you disagree with these scriptures or this line of thought, then you must find an answer for the following questions:

What happened to the large crowd of Holy ones who were resurrected with Jesus? Matthew 27:51
The scriptures say they will not go back into their graves. As Jesus said to the thief on the cross this day you will be with me in paradise.

Daniel 12:2 says And many of them that sleep in the dust of the earth, shall awake some to everlasting life and some to shame and everlasting contempt.

This scripture says, "cannot die anymore" so what

happened to the resurrected?

Luke 20:34 Jesus said to them, "Those who belong to this age marry and are given in marriage: V35 but those who are considered worthy of a place in that age and in the resurrection from the dead neither marry or are given in marriage V36 Indeed they cannot die anymore, because they are like angels and are the children of GOD, being children of the resurrection.

If Jesus took the thief with him don't you think he took the resurrected Holy ones, also? Luke 23:42 Then he said, "Jesus remember me when you come into your kingdom, Jesus answered him, "I tell you the truth, this day you will be with me in paradise."

Conclusion: Jesus Christ, is our High Priest and he fulfilled:
> the duties of the High Priest,
> the prophecies of the Torah, the Prophets, and
> the shadow pictures of the Feasts of Passover, Unleavened bread and First Fruits. The Lord's First Fruits wave offering was the "Holy ones" who were resurrected, the repentant thief on the cross, and the spotless lamb of the first year.

And he is coming back for you and me.

Part Four:
Timing of the Births of John the Baptist and Jesus Christ

What biblical evidence Supports, The Messiah, Jesus Christ being born on Christmas?

Ecclesiastes 3:15
> Whatever is has already been and
> What will be has been before, and
> GOD will call the past to account.

There are patterns in the Old Testament that need to be considered when studying the Feasts of GOD and the births of John, the Baptist, and Jesus Christ. The nation of Israel was delivered from Egypt after 430 years on the night of the first Passover.

Exodus 12:41 At the end of 430 years to the day, all the LORD's divisions left Egypt. Exodus 23:15 celebrate the Feast of Unleavened Bread (Passover) for seven days eat bread made without yeast as I have commanded you. Do this at the appointed time in the month of the Abib (Aviv) for in that month you came out of Egypt.

John, the Baptist, is born on Passover.

The lost period from Nehemiah to the New Testament is 430 years.

The end of Nehemiah 13:12 All Judah brought the tithes of grain, new wine, and oil into the storehouse.

This group of first fruits is an offering that happens at the Feast of Tabernacles. The date for this event is 433/432 BC Four hundred and thirty years (430) later 3/2 BC on the First day of the Feast of Tabernacles

Jesus Christ, The Messiah is born on the first day of the Feast of Tabernacles.

Biblical proofs for dating the births of Jesus Christ and John, the Baptist.

The Gospel of Luke gives us two details that give us a structure to date the birth of Jesus, (1). He tells us that Zechariah, father of John the Baptist, is in an order of priestly service that dates the exact date of the visit from the Angel Gabriel, and then (2) he tells us that Elizabeth (John's Mother) is 6 months pregnant when the Holy Spirit inseminates Mary. These two details give us an almost exact date. The conjunction of the dates with the celebration of GOD's Feast confirm the choreography of GOD and therefore:

1. John, the Baptist, is the fulfillment of the empty seat for the Prophet (in the Jewish family assumed to be for Elijah) left at the Passover table and

2. Jesus Christ tabernacled among us by being born at the Feast of Tabernacles.

There is no credible biblical evidence that Jesus was born

December 25, the date that 2,000 years ago was the winter solstice. The winter solstice was the shortest day of the year and attributed to the birthday of Mithra, Zeus, Jupiter, and other sun gods.

It is only fitting that the Christians celebrate Christmas to honor the only living GOD on December 25.

The detail given in the Gospel of Luke Allow us to date the birth of John the Baptist and Jesus Christ.

Sivan 9-10, 4BC Timing of Zechariah's meeting with the Angel, Gabriel.

Zechariah, of the priest (section / division) of Aviyah (Luke 1:5), while serving in the Temple burning incense to the Lord, the week after Pentecost, is visited by Gabriel, the angel who stands in the presence of Almighty GOD. Gabriel reveals, to Zechariah, GOD is giving him a son and to name him, John. To date this experience, we need to know about the scheduling of the priests. The Priests are divided into divisions. There were 24 divisions and their work schedule was based on one division each week was responsible for the Temple Services except during Feast weeks when all divisions worked. I Chronicles 24:10 Sets out the Divisions of the Priesthood and their service starting with the first full week of the Month of the Abib (Aviv) first month of the year.

Detail of the Priesthood Divisions work schedule
Starting after the first Sabbath
of the first month of the year
1st Week Yahoiariv division
Starting after the Sabbath after the new moon.
(Passover) All Divisions Serve
2nd Week Yedaiyah division
3rd Week Harim division
4th Week Seorim division
5th Week Malchiyah division
6th Week Miyamin division
7th Week Hakkoz division
(Shavuots / Pentecost) All Divisions Serve
8th Week Aviyah division (This is the division of Zechariah)

The reason we know that the meeting of Zechariah and Gabriel is the first day of the week, is that the scripture says there was a great multitude praying while Zechariah entered the Holy Place to burn the incense, this day is the High day ending The Pentecost Feast and the pilgrims will leave tomorrow.

Therefore, timing from the week after Pentecost: Aviyah division of Priesthood finishes service on the 16th day of Sivan and Zechariah starts travel to his home Luke 1:24 "and after these days Elizabeth conceives", 5th day of Tammuz 280 days (9 lunar months 10 days). This date is chosen because it fits with Gabriel's visit to Zechariah ,and to Mary, and Elizabeth being 6 months pregnant. And isn't it appropriate that the "light of the world" would be conceived during the Festival of Lights, Hanukkah.

Elizabeth's approximate date of conception & delivery of John the Baptist

Hebrew Months based on the lunar cycle 29.53 days per month
Tammuz 5th day (1) Partial month
Av (2) month of pregnancy
Elul (3) month of pregnancy
Tishri, (4) month of pregnancy
Heshwan (5) month of pregnancy
Kislev (6) month of pregnancy
Shevat (7) month of pregnancy
Teveth (8) month of pregnancy
Adar (9) month of pregnancy
Partial month Aviv (9) 14th Day

Birth of John the Baptist took place on Passover.

Isn't it appropriate that John the Baptist would be born on Passover, the day that we leave an empty place at the Passover Meal for the Prophet? Nisan 14/15, 3/2BC (Passover / Unleavened Bread), John the Baptist is born approximately 275 days after Gabriel visits Zechariah. IT IS JUST LIKE OUR GOD to put these little nuggets in the Bible to remind us that GOD is in charge of every detail.

Mary, Mother of Jesus, conception in the month of Teveth during Feast of Lights (Hanukkah)

Luke 1:28 Gabriel visits Mary and tells her she is highly favored! The Lord is with you.... Vs. 29...You will be with child and give birth to a son and you are to give him the name Jesus.... Vs. 38 I am the Lord's servant Mary answered, "May it be with me as you have said." Conception approximately the 2nd day of Teveth. Luke 1:36 Even Elizabeth, your relative, is going to have a child in her old age, and she, who was called barren, is in her sixth month. For nothing is impossible with GOD.

Therefore the Pregnancy of Mary is running six months after the conception of Elizabeth.

Hebrew Months based on the lunar cycle 29.53 days per month
Teveth (partial) month Mary's Conception at the end of the Feast of Lights (Hanukkah)
Shevat (2) month of pregnancy
Adar (3) month of pregnancy
Nisan (4) 14th Day
    Birth of John the Baptist on Passover
Iyyar (5) month of pregnancy
Sivan (6) month of pregnancy
Tammuz (7) month of pregnancy
Av (8) month of pregnancy

Elul (9) month of pregnancy
Tishri (partial) month 15th day.

Jesus Christ is born on the First day of Tabernacles, 15 Tishri.

Six months after the birth of John the Baptist, Jesus Christ, The Messiah, is born on the first day of the Feast of Tabernacles, eight days later on the Last Great Day, Jesus was dedicated and circumcised. This timing would align with custom of circumcision and dedication on the eighth day. The timing of the Feast, and Jesus being in the vicinity allowed his dedication to be at the Jerusalem Temple. Another confirmation of the birth and dedication date of Jesus Christ the Messiah, is the biblical references to the Prophecies of Simeon and Anna, prophets who seldom if ever left the Temple in Jerusalem.

Simeon's Prophecy: Luke 2:29
Sovereign Lord as you have promised
You now dismiss your servant in peace,
For my eyes have seen your salvation
Which you have prepared in the sight of all people
A light for revelation to the Gentiles
And for glory to your people Israel.

Therefore combining scripture with GOD's feast schedule gives us a clear picture of the timing and choreography of GOD's provision. Tishri 15, 3BC Birth of Jesus (High Sabbath of the Feast of Tabernacles)

John 1:14 "and the word became flesh and tabernacled among us", being born during the Feast of Tabernacles. The choice of words and the shadow pictures that are built in the Bible show us how much our GOD cares for us. Thirty years later during the "Offering and prayer for rain" on the last Great Day of the Feast of Tabernacles, Jesus yells as the High priest pours the water from the golden laver on the altar, " If any one thirst let him come un to me and drink, and I will give him living water. John 7:37

The timing of Jesus birth running six months later than The birth of John, the Baptist.

The date of Mary's conception being 6 months behind the pregnancy of Elizabeth, John the Baptists Mother. Mary asked the angel, Luke 1:34 "How will this be? since I am a virgin." The angel answered, "the Holy Spirit will come upon you and the Spirit of the Most High will overshadow you,"….V36 "Even your relative Elizabeth is going to have a child in her old age, and she who was said to be barren is in her 6th month. For nothing is impossible with GOD."

The heavens were alive with signs of the Lord's birth.

The Messiah's birth announcement to the shepherds was by an Angel and a Heavenly Host and they were told where to go. They did not follow a star. The shepherds saw the baby Jesus in the manger just after his birth.

The announcement to the Magi was a star sequence they had been waiting for their entire lives. My belief, The Prophet Daniel new the timing of the appearance of the Messiah, the Redeemer, and was in charge of teaching the Chaldeans (Magi) who studied the stars. We don't have scripture for the motivation and or the accumulation of the treasure, but we know that Daniel was a eunuch and had no heirs and it is possible he set up his wealth to be delivered to the young child, Jesus, for GOD's provision for the trip to Egypt. This scenario has another corroborating fact, the Chaldeans (Magi) had to ask where the Christ was born because they had seen his star in the rising, the prophecy of the Messiah being born in Bethlehem was not written for many years after the death of Daniel and Bethlehem was not a town yet. Ephrata was the name of the town before Bethlehem.

Astrological confirmation for the special star sequence seen by the Magi in Babylonia.

An hour and twenty minutes before Sunrise on Tishri 15, 3BC or August 12, 3BC on the Gregorian calendar: the planet Jupiter rose in conjunction with Venus, the morning star. This planetary alignment would have created a blazing light in the sky and then it went into retrograde motion and appeared to have stopped.

Matthew 2:1 now when Jesus was born in Bethlehem of Judea in the days of Herod the king, behold there came wise men from the east to Jerusalem.... Vs. 10 when they saw the star they rejoiced with exceeding great joy. The men from the East were as much as 700 miles away in Babylon (Persia) because the Bible says that "when they reached the house of the small child." Jesus was no longer a newborn and he was no longer in a manger but in a house.

Important note in verse 11 when the Chaldeans (Magi) arrive Jesus is a small child and has moved to a house.

Matthew 2:11 And when they were come into the house, they saw a young child with Mary, his mother, they fell down and worshipped him: and when they had opened their treasures they presented him with gifts: gold, frankincense and myrrh.
> **Myrrh** for The Lords death as our Savior.
> **Frankincense** for being our High Priest.
> **Gold** for our soon coming King.

Conclusion: The timing of the Births of Jesus Christ and John the Baptist lines up with scripture in John 2:20 and Luke 3:23, with signs in the sky, with the Daniel 9 Prophecy, and with the Roman Event commemorating Caesar Augustus' 25th year.

Details of the scriptural dating of the birth, baptism, and ministry of The Messiah Jesus Christ

John 2:20, about two months after his Baptism and at the Passover Feast. Jesus discovered merchants selling in the

Temple, he cleansed the Temple of merchants and their merchandise and was confronted by the Priests. The Priests and Pharisees said, "What miraculous sign can you show us to prove your authority to do all this?" Jesus answered them, "Destroy this Temple and I will raise it again in three days" The Jews replied, "you are going to rebuild the Temple in Three days and it has taken 46 years to build this Temple." But the Temple he had spoken of was his body. The Temple was started in 19/20 B.C. Therefore this Passover Feast was in the year 27 A.D. When you subtract 30 years from this Date the Birth of Jesus Christ happens 3/2 BC.

The Messiah, Jesus Christ age and ministry start is from Luke's' Gospel. Luke 3:23 when all the people were being baptized. Jesus was baptized too....vs.23 Now Jesus himself was about thirty years old when he began his ministry. The Greek word here is "hosei", meaning near but not yet attained. Not "peri", the Greek word for about, vicinity, a much broader term.

To agree with Daniel 9: The Messiah, the Anointed, one must enter the scene on the first day of the first month in 27 AD exactly 483 years after the decree for Ezra to leave Babylon to rebuild Jerusalem on the first day of the first month of 457 BC. (Ezra 7:9) It must be this year to line up with Jesus being 30 years of age and be in the right relationship to the age of the Temple from John 2:20

The Roman census or event commemorating Caesar

Augustus 25th year and given a new title (3/2 B.C.). Luke 2 There is no record of a census but many references to affirming the new title of Caesar as the Father of the Roman Empire (there were census in 8/7 BC and in 3/4 AD). This Roman Senate affirmation that Caesar Augustus is the Father of the Roman Empire would agree with the trip to Bethlehem for the birth of Jesus, This scenario allows The Messiah, Jesus Christ about 30 years old in 27 AD.

All of these dates line up with each other and confirm as a group of witnesses that Jesus was born in 3/2 BC and was age thirty in year 27 AD and died and was resurrected in 28 AD.

The End and the beginning, Aleph and Tav, Alpha and Omega.

Possible, plausible, and startling revelation for the third layer of Daniel 9

The Setting

May 14, 1948: On Saturday, The Sabbath, invitations went out for the Ceremony to Proclaim Independence of Israel at the Tel Aviv Museum. The invitations went out at 10:00 in the morning for late in the afternoon so as to not conflict with the Sabbath (Saturday May 14,1948)

Converting the 1947/1948 Gregorian calendar to the Sacred Calendar

According to GOD's Sacred Calendar, sundown May 14, 1948 begins the next day, the 6th day of Sivan (Hebrew 3rd month) which is the 50th day of counting of the omer, the High Sabbath of Pentecost (Shavuots).

Note: the Rabbinic calendar in use in Israel in 1948 recorded an extra month of Adar in 1947. The calculations for this decision are not based on barley crop grown in the Jerusalem area but instead on an arithmetic calculation of the extra month (7 times in 19 years) by the Rabbi's.

Using GOD's sacred calendar, without the Rabbi's arbitrary calculation, Israel became a nation on the High Sabbath of Pentecost, in one day.

Rebirth of Israel in one day

Isaiah 66:8 Who has ever heard of such a thing? Who has ever seen such things? Can a country be born in a day? Or a nation be brought forth in a moment? Yet no sooner is Zion in labor than she gives birth to her children....

Vs. 10 Rejoice with Jerusalem and be glad for her, all of you who love her: Rejoice greatly with her.

Note: the Seventy sevens, 490 day ministry of Jesus Christ, The Messiah, ended on the Sabbath before the High Sabbath of Pentecost. The Nation of Israel was birthed on the High Sabbath of Pentecost, the day after the Lord baptized the disciples and converts with the Holy Spirit and fire 1920 years before.

Does it seem more important to understand GOD's calendar?

www.ingramcontent.com/pod-product-compliance
Lightning Source LLC
Chambersburg PA
CBHW032105090426
42743CB00007B/237